ELIJAH
SPEAKS
TODAY

ELIJAH SPEAKS TODAY

THE LONG ROAD INTO NABOTH'S VINEYARD

G. GERALD HARROP

ABINGDON PRESS

NASHVILLE NEW YORK

ELIJAH SPEAKS TODAY

Copyright © 1975 by Abingdon Press

Library of Congress Cataloging in Publication Data

HARROP, G GERALD, 1917-
Elijah speaks today. 1. Elijah, the prophet. 2. Naboth
(Biblical character) 3. Bible. O.T. Prophets—Homi-
letical use. I. Title.
BS580.E4H33   251'.08   75-12755

ISBN 0-687-11654-6

Scripture quotations noted RSV are from the Revised
Standard Version of the Bible, copyrighted 1946, 1952,
and 1971, by the Division of Christian Education, National Council of Churches, and are used by permission.

Scripture quotations noted NAB are from the New
American Bible.

MANUFACTURED BY THE PARTHENON PRESS AT
NASHVILLE, TENNESSEE, UNITED STATES OF AMERICA

DEDICATION

This brief account of one prophet's response to an event in his time was conceived, written, reflected upon, and revised between October, 1973, and November, 1974. During that time truly momentous events were taking place: the Yom Kippur war and the ensuing oil embargo, the unfolding of the Watergate drama with its dénouement in the resignation of President Nixon and his pardon by President Ford. In Ulster the fratricide continued in its terrible course, and all of us became conscious of the mounting population and food crisis, which was taking on apocalyptic proportions. Our dialogue with the prophetic word in scripture proceeds simultaneously on two levels: the prophet's conversation both with his own time and (through us) with ours. We do not abstract "doctrines" from the prophetic scriptures and apply them to our time and place. Rather we try to hear the Word of God for our time in the prophet's word for his. This is a kind of complicated hermeneutic, and what follows is an attempt to

5

demonstrate how it can work out in terms of a single passage of the prophetic scriptures—I Kings 21. The reader will live already in a different time from the writer, so swiftly does the course of history run in our global village.

My friend and former student Gary N. Johnston prepared the character descriptions and dialogue (and very much improved the plot from my original suggestion!) for the dramatic presentation that is chapter 5. I am grateful especially to him, but also to all my students, past and present, not only for their contributions to my understanding but for their very presence, which reminds me that to understand the prophetic response in antiquity is but the first step on the way to a prophetic ministry.

Nathaniel H. Parker, now retired in Mississippi, was the teacher who first awakened my interest in the Hebrew language and the Old Testament scriptures. If I am a "son of the prophets" he is one of my fathers!

To my wife, Freda, I owe much more than gratitude for the careful preparation of the manuscript and its several revisions.

G. GERALD HARROP

Mid-Lent, 1975

CONTENTS

I The Development of the Elijah Saga Cycle

In the ancient Near East many little nations rose and fell. For a time they flourished while the great empires about them were temporarily weak or occupied elsewhere. But for each of them the day of doom inevitably dawned and they disappeared, not only as living communities and political entities, but also from the notice and memory of mankind. Of these nations, as of their inhabitants, the poetic obituary stands:

> For the wind passeth over it, and it is gone;
> And the place thereof shall know it no more.

In the year 722/21 B.C. the city of Samaria fell to the Assyrian emperor and warlord Sargon II; with the fall of its capital the northern Hebrew kingdom, Israel, passed into what might well have been the dim limbo of barely remembered ancient history. Countless pieces of broken pottery and a few more imposing human artifacts mark the place of its settlements. Royal annals and war diaries somehow survived. Not on their account, however, but on account of the stories of the messengers or prophets of the little nation's God, does Israel live still. For the god of this obscure people has become for many the God of the whole world, and his prophets have become spokesmen to the generations and to the nations. The stories of these prophets were told; they were written down; they were collected; they were incorporated into books which have become Bible. So they live, and Israel lives. We cannot tell when these stories were first told, when they were written down, when they were collected. Very likely the collection did not occur until Judah alone remained the custodian of the traditions of ancient Israel.

When Amos and Hosea came on the scene in the eighth century, their oracles (poetic, prophetic messages) were soon written down, probably by scribes in their disciple circle. Thus we know them by their own words. But their predecessors—such men as Nathan, Gad, Micaiah ben Imlah, Elisha and, above all, Elijah—we know only through stories told about them. From these stories it is clear that the greatest of the preclassical [1] prophets was Elijah. In fact, Elijah became for Israel the model prophet, the paradigm of prophecy, whom the Lord took to himself to heaven (II Kings 2:1-12) that he might send him back to announce the dawn of the messianic age (Mal. 4:5-6). In the Gospel vision of the glorified Messiah it is Elijah who represents prophecy even as Moses represents law (Mark 9:2-8 and parallels).

What manner of man lies behind the sagas and legends that make Elijah supremely *the* prophet in the generations and centuries that followed? Can we penetrate behind these stories and learn anything about this man? This is a difficult task because the persons who told these stories and wrote them down, and even the editors who collected them, do not seem to have been interested in even the most basic biographical data. We are told that Elijah came from Tishbe in Gilead.[2] But we are not told anything about his ancestry, although genealogy is very important almost everywhere in the Old Testament. He is established in neither time nor place in a very exact way. He appears from the desert, dressed in typical desert garb, does the divine deed and utters the prophetic word, then seems almost to be snatched away, disappearing as a slight white craft is swallowed up in a sea fog. As one of his anxious and more settled colleagues put it: "As soon as I have gone from you, the Spirit of the Lord will carry you whither I know not" (I Kings 18:12 RSV).

The stories about Elijah are found in that tract of scripture which begins abruptly at I Kings 17:1 and ends with the story of his final disappearance in II Kings 2:14. If you take from this long passage two chapters—I Kings 20 and 22—you have the Elijah saga-cycle. This is the collection of stories about Elijah. There survive in Scripture eleven of these stories.

1) Elijah is fed by ravens in a great drought (I Kings 17:1-7).
2) At the home of the widow of Zarephath, Elijah is miraculously sustained by a wonder jar and cruse (I Kings 17:8-16).
3) The reviving of the woman's son, who is apparently dead (I Kings 17:17-24).
4) Elijah and Obadiah (I Kings 18:1-16).
5) The ordeal on Mount Carmel (I Kings 18:17-40).
6) The end of the drought (I Kings 18:41-46).
7) Elijah's flight from Jezebel's anger to Horeb (I Kings 19:1-18).
8) Recruitment of Elisha (I Kings 19:19-21).
9) The story of Naboth's vineyard (I Kings 21:1-29).
10) Judgment on Ahaziah (II Kings 1:1-18).
11) The ascension of Elijah (II Kings 2:1-14).

The first six of these stories are connected with

a three-year drought in the reign of Ahab, whose regnal dates are 869–850 B.C.[3] The next three are also associated with the reign of Ahab, the last two are set in the times of his sons and immediate successors, Ahaziah (850–849) and Jehoram (849–842). The probability is that the appearances of Elijah to Israel occurred in the decade and a half beginning in about 865.

The context of the Elijah stories is the account of the eternal struggle of the faith of Israel against the religion and culture of Canaan. The Israelite tribes had brought into Palestine the faith of their nomadic ancestors. It was a religion and ethos as sparce and stern as the desert that had spawned it. Their god, Yahweh, [4] had delivered them from Egyptian slavery. He had sustained a whole generation of them in the desert wasteland that lies between Egypt and Canaan, a forbidding and bleak area that is once again much in the news. Their covenant, or agreement, with him involved for them obedience to his law in exchange for his favor and protection. The first article of that law was the total prohibition of any worship or tribute to be paid to any god save Yahweh, he being a jealous god. Because other gods were represented by sculpture and pictures, the Israelite was forbidden to make any likeness of any god, and this even included Yahweh himself. If a tourist had entered an Israelite shrine, whether a primitive portable shrine in the desert or the very temple of Solomon, he would have asked in amazement, "Where is the god of this shrine?"

Yahweh had made himself known to Israel by acting decisively and redemptively in the nation's history at the moments of great emergency and crisis. He delivered them from Egypt. He sustained them in the desert. He led them into the promised land and gave them victory over their foes. The land was his gift. Its produce was his gift.[5] The fruit of the land could not be wrung from its stubborn soil by acts of religious magic. Yahweh gives. Yahweh withholds. All good gifts—grain or fruit, animals or offspring—are the gifts of Yahweh, who is the lord of all life. He will give to his own people if his law is obeyed, and at the head of this law is his sole jealous claim to worship and allegiance: "You shall have no other god before me" (RSV).

The people were bound to this one god, and in their covenant with him they were bound just as inexorably to one another. This has been the heart of Israel's faith down the centuries. "You shall love the Lord your God with all your heart, and with all your soul, and with all your mind. This is the great and first commandment. And a second is like it, You shall love your neighbor as yourself. On these two commandments depend all the law and the prophets." (Matt. 22:37-40 RSV.) Israel was the people of Yahweh. Each Israelite was his brother's keeper. The leaders of the nation

14

—be they patriarchs, judges, or kings—were not exempt from the obligation to God and brother. They themselves were gifts of Yahweh to his people for an immediate task. When the task was done they were removed lest they exalt themselves against their God and above their fellows. He gave them Moses, and he took him away as they were about to enter the promised land. He raised up Joshua and the judges. They were the instruments of his grace and the rods of his anger. In early, pre-monarchic Israel no man was a leader in his own right, whether that right be by inheritance or by military and political power. Of king and commander, wife and children, grain and fruit, ox and ass, water, fertility, prosperity, victory it was said: "Yahweh gives, and Yahweh takes away: blessed be the name of Yahweh."

When they entered the promised land, the invading desert tribes found nations, cultures, religions, and customs older than their own, tested by the use of the centuries in that place. For these nations and their customs were not obliterated by the invading Israelites, although they seemed to remember a divine command to exterminate utterly—to practice genocide.[6] Indeed some later interpreters of Israel's history blamed the nation's problems on its failure to exterminate—to carry the holy war to its "final solution"—to obliterate the people of the land and all material evidence of its existence (I Sam. 15:10 ff.). But

15

this was manifestly impossible, and the Canaanite way of life persisted, a perpetual threat and temptation to Israel's faith, uniqueness, and very existence.

Ancient Canaanitish baalism is a religion that is almost impossible to limit and define with any degree of precision. It resembles Hinduism somewhat in this respect. It is a religion and life-style based on the intuition and conviction that humans must somehow relate to, imitate, and appease the mysterious powers that undergird, surround, and rule over them, giving them life and the means of its perpetuation. This is done by relating ritualistically to these powers, who are sometimes personalized and represented as lords, gods, husbands—the baalim. Fertility is obviously connected with sex, so sacred prostitution—union with "holy" people attached to god and shrine—is part of this religious practice. Most prominent of all, of course, is the worship of gods who are represented by images and pictures.

The political power that sustains the social order is part of this grand scheme. The king rules by an inherent divine right, and his mysterious presence and power is part of the universal divine order. He must be appeased and flattered. Religion is the means by which the totality of this grand scheme is comprehended and perpetuated. Man participates in the activity of the gods. The temptation to become part of this near-universal style and spirit is the perpetual temptation of Israel, a testing which she can never leave forever behind her. From the days of the judges (about 1100) to the days of the Maccabees (170) nothing has really changed although the Greeks from Europe have now replaced the Canaanites from Asia. "In those days there appeared in Israel men who were breakers of the law, and they seduced many people, saying 'Let us go and make an alliance with the Gentiles all around us; since we separated from them, many evils have come upon us.' The proposal was agreeable; some from among the people promptly went to the king, and he authorized them to introduce the way of living of the Gentiles. Thereupon they built a gymnasium in Jerusalem according to the Gentile custom. They covered over the mark of their circumcision and abandoned the holy covenant; they allied themselves with the Gentiles and sold themselves to wrongdoing." (I Macc. 1:11-15 NAB.)

At a very critical moment in the struggle of Yahweh with the baalim, the prophet Elijah appeared. For in Jezebel, princess of Tyre and dynamic wife of Israel's king Ahab, a champion of the baalim came to a position of power and influence. Jezebel was determined to impose the advanced religion and culture of the ancient Canaanite city-states on the barbarous subjects of her husband. She realized that to do this she would have to rid the land of its jealous god and his fanatical prophets. So she established, near the seat of power, a shrine to baal, and she supported at her court many prophets of baal. In the memory of Israel she became the seductress supreme who incited her husband to sin against Yahweh (I Kings 21:25). Elijah opposed her and in so doing set in motion the forces that ultimately destroyed Jezebel and the dynasty of her husband (II Kings 9:30 ff.). Baalism was not wiped out; it was never to be wiped out—but neither was Yahwism. The faith of Israel survived Jezebel and in so doing surmounted perhaps its supreme temptation. For she had behind her all the political, religious, and cultural resources of the civilized and settled part of the ancient Near East that we call the Fertile Crescent. Elijah, the prophet of the resistance, became at the time of the hottest battle "the chariots of Israel, and the horsemen thereof" (II Kings 2:12).

Elijah is remembered in the collection of stories told about him. Of these stories, and no doubt there were many of them, the eleven listed above found their way into scripture. It is important for us to realize that each of these stories was told originally on its own and carried its message. They answer some questions about Elijah. How did he, living in the most arid part of the country, survive the great drought that devastated the land in the reign of Ahab? In one story he is fed by ravens (I Kings 17:4), [7] in another he is befriended

18

by the widow of Zarephath; the prophet, his hostess, and her son are sustained by the wonder jar and cruse whose flour and oil mysteriously replenish themselves (I Kings 17:16). In another story we find the prophet reviving his hostess' apparently dead son by a method that seems to resemble oral resuscitation—the so-called kiss of life (I Kings 17:17-24).[8] These stories are a particular kind of saga. Some scholars call them "legends"—tales told of a holy man which illustrate the wonder and mystery of the divine presence in his life. Because they have no public consequences but are purely personal these stories are not as important and historically interesting as stories which show his role in the political and religious struggles of his time.[9]

In the story of Elijah and Obadiah (I Kings 18:1-16) we move toward the historically more interesting type of narrative. We see in this story that Ahab retained at least one faithful Yahweh prophet in his entourage—the "reform" of Jezebel was not 100 percent. Elijah uses Obadiah to make possible a meeting with Ahab and to set the stage for the most dramatic of the Elijah stories—the contest on Mount Carmel which culminated in the slaughter, instigated by Elijah, of 450 Jezebel-sponsored baal prophets. (I Kings 18:17-40). In the short story which follows, Elijah tells Ahab to flee from the mountain for the drought is coming to an end in a violent storm (I King 18:41-46).

19

In the seventh story, Elijah flees from Jezebel's anger and fury on a forty-day foot journey to Mount Horeb, the traditional site of Yahweh's original covenant with Israel. This story is hard to understand in its present context. For at the climax of the Carmel contest, the people support Elijah the vindicated champion of Yahweh crying, "Yahweh, he is God"; then join him in slaughtering the prophets of baal (I Kings 18:39-40). But now, unaccountably, Elijah feels isolated and alone in his fidelity and his danger (I Kings 19:10). It is only when we realize that each story was first told on its own that we can understand this sequence. At Horeb Elijah receives the revelation of the "still small voice (I Kings 19:12) [10] which tells him of his role in the coming judgment on Ahab's dynasty: he will anoint the prophet who will inspire it and the soldier who will carry it out (I Kings 19:15-18). After a short legend-type story introducing us to Elijah's prophetic successor (I Kings 19:19-21) we have the narrative which will become the focus of our inquiry—the story of the confiscation of Naboth's vineyard. Let us notice at once that this story is very different. It is no pious legend about Elijah in any way, shape, or form. For Elijah does no marvelous deed either to save Naboth or avenge him. Jezebel's evil deed reaps its intended reward and Naboth dies, his family robbed of its sacred land. Elijah has but one function here. He utters the prophetic, judgmental word of Yahweh. The final two stories in our sequence are highly legendary and marvelous, describing the judgment of Ahaziah (Ahab's successor) (II Kings 1) and the ascension of Elijah, who disappears as mysteriously as he arrived (II Kings 2:1-12).

There are, then, two kinds of Elijah story. We have the kind of anecdote that arises about any great, legendary hero (like the Washington's cherry tree story), and we have narratives that illuminate his role in history. In Elijah's case his destiny was to confront Ahab and Jezebel. The two great, classic stories of this confrontation are the account of the contest on Mount Carmel with the prophets of baal and the story of Naboth's judicial murder by Ahab and Jezebel. These stories are obviously of more interest to us than the pious anecdotes. Both reflect the tremendous power in verbal artistry that characterized the early Hebrew narrators. Whether these accounts were written down from the beginning (the Succession Document—II Sam. 9–20; I Kings 1–2) or have a pre-literary oral history, they tell their tale with a kind of word economy and a vivid sense of place, person, and motion that is almost unique in literature. The Hebrew language, as rich in verbs of action and nouns of substance as it is poor in abstract nouns and adjectives, was admirably suited to their purpose of simply telling the story of what happened, where, and to whom—almost letting the story carry itself without comment or moralizing. When the writer of the Succession Document pauses in his vivid tale of David's lust and treachery to say, "The thing that David did displeased Yahweh" (II Sam. 11:27), the power of the few simple words is worth a million of the painful, moralizing observations so dear to the heart of his deuteronomic editor, who fortunately kept his hands off the story at that point.

In the story of the Carmel contest there is an element of high humor. We can imagine the glee which greeted the teller of the tale when he comes to the place where Elijah pokes cruel fun at the hapless prophets whose god would not respond to their increasingly desperate plea: "Yell at him —louder! After all he is a god! Perhaps he is day dreaming, or resting, or maybe he has gone to the privy! Maybe he has dozed off and you will have to wake him up!" (I Kings 18:27. Freely, but accurately, translated.) But the unfortunate "spiritual leaders," stung by these taunts of their adversary, "called out louder and slashed themselves with swords and spears, as was their custom, until blood gushed over them. Noon passed and they remained in a prophetic state until the time for offering sacrifice. But there was not a sound: no one answered, and no one was listening." (I Kings 18:28-29 NAB.)

In the story of Naboth's vineyard, Elijah is not the central figure. He appears only after the dire

22

deed is done and announces the judgment of Yahweh—the coming doom of Ahab, Jezebel, and the
whole house of Omri. The story is totally without
sign and wonder, save the sign of the word of the
prophet. No *deus ex machina* rescues the unfortunate Naboth. The story is kept alive in the memory
of the people because of this prophetic word. This
word is itself happening—it is doom and judgment
—for it is the Word of God. The story is placed
where we find it in the Hebrew Bible, and hence
in the English translations, just before the account
of Ahab's last battle and death before Ramoth-
Gilead.[11]

If we combine the passage I Kings 16: 29-32 with
I Kings 22: 39-40, we have the skeleton outline of
the reign of Ahab:

> In the thirty-eighth year of Asa, king of Judah,
> Ahab, son of Omri, became king of Israel; he reigned
> over Israel in Samaria for twenty-two years. Ahab,
> son of Omri, did evil in the sight of the Lord more
> than any of his predecessors. It was not enough for
> him to imitate the sins of Jeroboam, son of Nebat.
> He even married Jezebel, daughter of Ethbaal, king
> of the Sidonians, and went over to the veneration
> and worship of Baal. Ahab erected an altar to Baal
> in the temple of Baal which he built in Samaria,
> and also made a sacred pole. He did more to anger
> the Lord, the God of Israel, than any of the kings
> of Israel before him. . . . The rest of the acts of
> Ahab, with all that he did, including the ivory palace
> and all the cities he built, are recorded in the book
> of the chronicles of the kings of Israel. Ahab rested

23

with his ancestors, and his son Ahaziah succeeded
him as king. [NAB]

In the immediately preceding passage, I Kings
16:23-28, the historian tells the story of Omri,
Ahab's father and founder of the dynasty, in fewer
words than this, although Omri was probably the
most important ruler in Israel's history from the
standpoint of world history. In fact the country
was called Omriland in Assyrian records for a
great many years after he and his dynasty had
passed away. In the case of Ahab the usual formula
for describing the reigns of Israel's kings has had
inserted into it a great deal of material. Apart
from the strange little note at 16:34, and two battle
accounts (chaps. 20 and 22), the interpolated material consists of stories of the prophets—mostly
stories of the prophet Elijah. The Elijah cycle of
stories consists of eleven which were written down
and shaped into a continuous narrative. That this
narrative may have once been longer and contained
some biographical information is indicated in the
abrupt way the prophet is introduced at 17:1.

Ahab's reign receives this massive extra attention because of a serious drought and famine in
the early years of his reign, a critical war with
neighbors to the northeast and, above all, the decisive religious confrontation personified in the
figures of Elijah and Jezebel. Persons unknown,
and indeed unknowable to us, selected and
arranged the stories of Elijah that seemed to

24

them to be most interesting, most dramatic, most entertaining (for the stories were first of all *told*), most significant. They were put in roughly chronological order and then perhaps incorporated in a longer narrative of prophetic stories which included tales of Elijah's predecessors and successors. The deuteronomic historian took this narrative and for the most part left it as it came to him; for some happy reason he let both the prophetic narrator of the Elijah stories and the writer of the Succession Document have their say in their own words and way. Thus there has been preserved for us some of the most powerful and vivid word pictures that we have in all scripture. So the writers put the Elijah stories and the battle narratives (and other prophetic stories such as the Micaiah narrative in chap. 22) into the framework of Ahab's reign, which in turn has its place in their long, solemn, sad, majestic account of Israel's march from rebellion to doom. In their mind Ahab's reign illustrates why Israel was doomed—why Yahweh would turn away from her even before he turned away from her apostate sister Judah. In their great work, which stretches from the death of Moses (Josh. 1:1) about 1250 to the fall of Jerusalem (II Kings 25) in 587, all history is comprehended in the dictum that for man and nation, even for the nation of God's choosing, what is deserved and what finally happens is weighed in the balance and found equal.

25

2 the search for the historical elijah

The reign of Ahab was very critical for the theological interpretation of Israel's history that has survived in our Bible. For above all his wretched predecessors and successors, Ahab, incited by his wife Jezebel, caused Israel to sin and hastened her doom (I Kings 21:25). Ahab has the historical misfortune to be presented to us in a context dominated by a theological viewpoint hostile to him. What can we learn about persons whom we meet only in the words of their enemies?

Yet if we abandon the search for the historical Ahab, and thus the historical Elijah, on this account, we will be driven into agnosticism about all history and will have to conclude, with Henry Ford, that "history is bunk." We have neither tape nor photograph from antiquity. The faces we see and the words we hear come from reporters, from other human beings. And no human being took the trouble to tell or write the story without a motive for so doing. As far as we know there were no royalties!

Much of what we know about the great men of antiquity, the leaders of nations, comes from court scribes whose business was flattery. The annals of the kings of Egypt and Mesopotamia are exercises in literary glorification. We are, I think, rather more fortunate in the case of ancient Israel. As biased as the picture may be in the hands and mouths of theological critics, it would be more so if we had only the record of court apologists. The deuteronomic historians and editors were keen propagandists for their viewpoint—that Israel prospered when she was true to Yahweh and free of idolatry, and suffered when she forsook the covenant and turned to other gods. But they were not dishonest. They did not have to be dishonest.

It was politically prudent for Ahab to seek accommodation with the culture, politics, and religion of the world about him. His father had arranged the marriage of his son with a Tyrian princess for this purpose and, politically and militarily speaking, it was a wise purpose. From the standpoint of political and military results it could be argued that Omri and Ahab were Israel's wisest rulers (including the rulers of both kingdoms) after David. This accommodation included some sort of entente with the nature religion of Palestine and Syria. That Ahab did not intend to forsake Yahweh can be seen in his children's names—Ahaziah and Jehoram. Both of these names are compounded from "Yahweh." For Ahab the Yahweh-Baal contest need not be "either-or"; it could be "both-and." There is no reason to doubt that his Tyrian wife would encourage his opening to baalism and denigrate his residual ancestral faith.

Nor is there any reason to doubt the historicity of the spokesman of Yahwism. For the Yahweh of the ancestral, desert faith does not move into pantheons—"for I, Yahweh your God, am a jealous God. You shall have no other gods in my presence" (Exod. 20:2-4). And throughout Israel's history, there were prophets and religious orders which stood for the ancient faith, the eternal covenant with a jealous God. Thus conflict was incipient and inevitable in the situation in which Ahab found himself. There was no need for the deuteronomist to turn novelist here. The facts did not have to be *much* rearranged or bent to support him.

Yet we must also recognize the truth that by

a different selection, emphasis, and arrangement of the facts, and a context of editorial comment more favorable to Ahab, we could have an account of his reign which would present him as, on the whole, a wise and prudent ruler. This could be done and the story would still be essentially true. For even in the context we do have, the good things about Omri and Ahab can be discerned. In the two centuries (922–721 B.C.) of the northern kingdom's wretched history, the short period of Omride rule (876–842) was an interlude of at least gray light in a night of thick darkness. In this period the fortified citadel of the capital city, Samaria, was secured and built. Israel's neighbors to the immediate northeast were contained, and indeed Damascus became an ally in an anti-Assyrian alliance. Thus a grave threat to Israel's very existence was removed. The Assyrian conquest of Samaria was not to occur for more than a century. Had Ahab been succeeded by sons as able as his father and himself, Israel might have enjoyed the kind of continuity and legitimacy of dynastic government that the Davidic line secured for Judah and, like her, might have survived the Assyrian menace.

Our basic source for the story of ancient Israel to 587 is the so-called deuteronomic history:

In the Old Testament one must mention first of all the great historical work which comprises the books

29

of Deuteronomy, Joshua, Judges, Samuel, Kings, which we call "deuteronomistic" by reason of its language and spirit, and which offers the very first exposition of the "history of Israel" up to the events of the year 587 B.C. The author of this compilation passed on numerous sources from different periods, of different extent and different origin and nature, partly *in extenso,* partly in extracts, and developed the whole work from these sources. He thereby conveyed to posterity a mass of valuable traditional material and without his work we should know very little about the earlier phases of the history of Israel.[1]

As Noth points out here, this long deuteronomic history incorporates sources that antedate it. These sources include royal and military diaries, victory poems, dirges, and early narratives. Among these earlier narratives was the Elijah saga-cycle, which in turn was made up of stories about Elijah originally told separately. Another source is an account of Ahab's wars with Aram, an account which was pro-Ahab.[2] For the reign of Ahab, then, there have been preserved for us at least two early predeuteronomic sources—one (the Elijah cycle) anti-Ahab, the other (a war diary) pro-Ahab. For few other periods are we so well served with early material.

The first king of the united tribes was Saul (about 1020–1000); he was succeeded by David (1000–960), who deposed him. In his rise to power David was supported by the seer Samuel, who turned away from Saul although he had anointed him as the first king. David not only became king but became the first father of a dynasty—something new for Israel, which had hitherto depended upon charismatic leaders who emerged (theological interpretation said they were raised up by Yahweh) in emergencies and crises. In II Samuel 7 we have a source called "the oracle of Nathan," which gives us the prophetic and religious authorization of the Davidic dynasty. In the long narrative II Samuel 9–20 and I Kings 1–2 we have an ancient account of David's court and family. The purpose of this narrative is to set forth the story of how David came to be succeeded by Solomon, who was neither his first son nor really legitimate, being the child of his famous father's criminal, murderous lust. This narrative, incorporated with little change into the deuteronomic narrative, is the outstanding piece of historical writing in the whole Bible— perhaps in all antiquity. Its unknown author has a good claim to be "the father of history." He stood close to the scene and called the shots as he saw them, without regard to the favor of either king or priest. Because of him there is no need to engage in a search for the historical David. We know David better than we know anyone else in all antiquity!

But the establishment of a dynastic monarchy, patterned on the political institutions of the great nations around them, was by no means accepted

31

by all the people. Some of them and some of their prophets saw it as a falling away from immediate dependence upon the god of Israel, who was their only true king. He could be depended upon to send leaders as the need arose, and remove them lest they become tyrants and gods. Moreover the new order was made visible by a government and civil service centralized in Jerusalem (a capital selected by David, who captured it from the Cananites; it was thus not an ancient holy shrine) and separated from the people by distance and by the presence of a growing bureaucracy which kept them from their king. The coming rebellion could be seen in two revolts which occurred during David's lifetime (II Sam. 15:1 ff. and II Sam. 20:1-2). Although both were put down, they were portents of things to come. In the reign of Solomon there emerged the rebel who was to destroy united Israel.

Jeroboam, the son of Nebat, a Solomonic labor leader from the Joseph tribes, encouraged by a prophet named Ahijah, moved against Solomon but was detected and had to flee to Egypt, where he awaited the death of Solomon and the accession of his son Rehoboam (I Kings 11:26-40). When Rehoboam tried to continue and intensify his father's oppression and tyranny, Jeroboam struck, and the people of ten tribes followed him into secession. The new "northern" kingdom, Israel, was founded. The house of David was left with the

32

territory of Judah, the environs of Jerusalem, and eventually controlled much of the territory that had been assigned to Benjamin. Its strength lay in its isolation from the normal path of world conquerors and its acceptance of the concept of dynastic legitimacy. This gave it a sense of continuity that Israel, whose kings were little more than charismatic "judges,"[3] never attained. The Davidic state was called Judah.

But Jeroboam's new state was much larger, richer in resources, and more important strategically and commercially. This, of course, was both its opportunity and its mortal danger. It was coveted by the great powers of Mesopotamia and Egypt, while Judah almost had to expose itself deliberately to be harrassed and invaded.[4] But the age of viability for *ad hoc* charismatic leadership had passed. Israel rarely enjoyed stable government. The wonder is that it lasted two centuries (922–721). During that time it suffered eight dynastic changes; these were usually accompanied by bloody purges.

The deuteronomic historians attributed this instability to Israel's inherent religious infidelity. While Davidic Judah had a few good and loyal believing kings, Israel had none. They all "walked in the way of Jeroboam the son of Nebat who made Israel to sin."[5] Of this sorry lot Ahab, the son of Omri, was, according to the deuteronomic historian, the sorriest of all—"there was none who sold himself to do what was evil in the sight of the Lord like Ahab, whom Jezebel his wife incited" (I Kings 21:25 RSV).

The first half-century of Israel's existence (about 922–876) was a time of extreme instability. "Jeroboam . . . had, like Saul, come to power through prophetic designation and subsequent acclamation by the people, presumably in covenant. Kingship in Israel was in theory charismatic: by divine designation and popular consent. But a real return to charismatic leadership was impossible."[6]

Jeroboam's son, Nadab (901–900), was assassinated by one of his officers, called Baasha, who held power during his lifetime (900–877; I Kings 15:27–16:6). But Baasha's son, Elah, could not retain the throne—he was assassinated by one of his officers, called Zimri (I Kings 16:9), who held power only a few days. When the army general Omri moved on Tirzah, the temporary capital (I Kings 16:16, 17), Zimri committed suicide (I Kings 16:18). After a few years of chaos, Omri not only established himself, but founded a dynasty that lasted to the third generation from 876 to 842 (I Kings 16:22–II Kings 9:24). The Omride dynasty then gave a short period of thirty-four years of stability. It ended with the bloodiest of all purges, led by Elisha and Jehu. In the long reign of Jeroboam II, 786–746, nearly a century later, Israel had another relatively long period of prosperity and stability. It is interesting to note that both ostensibly happy periods

34

were the eras of the most intense prophetic attack and criticism. The Omrides were confronted by Elijah and Elisha; Jeroboam II had to contend with Amos and Hosea.

Omri and his son Ahab were undoubtedly Israel's best rulers. They dealt promptly and seriously with the real problems that confronted them. There were four main problems:

1) The nation had neither permanent capital nor continuing dynasty. Its government, then, was not secure in place and time.
2) In the first half-century of its existence it had frittered away its energies in border disputes with Judah.
3) To the immediate northeast the Aramean kingdom of Damascus threatened the nation's borders and its very existence.
4) There loomed above the little nations of the eastern Mediterranean the mortal threat of a resurgent Assyrian empire.

Even the hostility of the deuteronomic editor-writer does not conceal from us the fact that considerable success was enjoyed by Omri and Ahab in dealing with all four problems. Ahab was able to succeed his father without incident and pass the throne on to his sons. He continued the building and fortification of Samaria, the capital site purchased by Omri. It was a good site—elevated and defensible, convenient in location, yet not connected with one tribe as against the others. In this the Omride selection of Samaria was like David's choice of Jerusalem. Border disputes with Judah seem to have been settled—indeed Judah became an ally in the Aramean wars (I Kings 22:1-4). Early in Ahab's reign his "daughter" Athaliah was married to the Judean crown prince Jehoram, thus cementing the alliance (II Kings 8:18).[7] Ahab's own marriage to Jezebel had been arranged to ally Israel with the commercially important coastal city and area of Tyre, and to secure the friendship of that city and its king and thus counterbalance the threat from Damascus. Though the reports of the war with Damascus preserved for us in I Kings 20 and 22 reflect only mixed success for Ahab, the fact is that Israel did not succumb to her stronger rival. In 853 we find Israel allied with Damascus and other neighboring states in a coalition which apparently succeeded in stopping Shalmaneser III and the Assyrians at Qarqar on the Orontes river in Syria. Here Israel emerges on the pages of world history in the Assyrian records of Shalmaneser:

> I departed from Argana and approached Karkara. I destroyed, tore down and burned down Karkara, his royal residence. He brought along to help him 1,200 chariots, 1,200 cavalrymen, 20,000 foot soldiers of Adad-'idri (i.e. Hadadezer) of Damascus . . . , 700 chariots, 700 cavalrymen, 10,000 foot soldiers of Irhuleni from Hamath, 2,000 chariots, 10,000 foot soldiers of Ahab, the Israelite. . . .[8]

Although Qarqar must have been the most important event of Ahab's reign, it is not mentioned in the Bible. The Assyrians certainly remember the Omrides, since Shalmaneser III (842), Adanari IV (about 792), and Tiglath-Pileser III (733–32) all call Israel *Omriland.* [9]

Jezebel was the daughter of Ethbaal (or Ittobaal) the king of Tyre—called correctly the king of the Sidonians, for the older city of Sidon gave its name to the region which included Tyre. Ethbaal was a priest of Astarte, who was either the mother or consort of the Tyrian god Melcarth (spelled also Melkart, or Melqart).[10] When the book of Kings speaks of Baal, using this epithet as a personal name, the god referred to is Melqart, the local baal or lord. Jezebel's name seems to mean "Where is the baal?" which is a kind of cultic cry.[11] She was undoubtedly a zealous missionary for her own god, and she intended to extend his sway to Israel. Her religion

with its epidemic ecstaticism, its colorful ritual of fertility, and probably its picturesque initiations . . . stood in sharp contrast to the sober hues and stern morality of Yahwism, even when the latter was made more palatable to the common man by sacrificial ritual and solemn chants. Elijah and Elisha threw themselves with unexampled ardor into the conflict and won a signal triumph. The menace of Melcarth was definitely exorcised, and with its elimination Yahwism triumphed at last over the direct onslaught of Baalism. [12]

37

Although they were mortal foes, Ahab and Elijah guaranteed each other's memory in history. It was the incorporation of the Elijah stories into the deuteronomic history that kept the name of Ahab alive more than the names of Israel's other kings. And, ironically, it probably made his reign important enough that the deuteronomist also incorporated the war reports that sometimes reflect with credit on Ahab's character and courage. At the same time it is the attestation to Ahab and the Omrides in the Assyrian records, the Moabite stone,[13] and the material remains of the city of Samaria that solidifies the otherwise legendary prophet into a flesh-and-blood historical figure. The mortal challenge to the faith of Israel called for an Elijah. The survival of Yahwism, despite the gravity and power of its opposition in the ninth century, testifies to the reality and power of his presence. We may concede that some of the stories told about him are pious anecdotes which may or may not have some basis in fact. But we really do not need to know that Elijah was fed by ravens or by a wonder jar and cruse, or even what kind of event is reflected in the strange and wondrous account of his ascension. What interests us is the kind of story that remembers him as the champion of the ancient faith of Israel in the face of an overwhelming temptation for the people to merge and melt into the common religion, culture, and

38

political system of the stronger nations around about them.

The prophetic movement which the life and words and deeds of Elijah inspired rallied the forces of Yahwism and hastened the doom of the powerful house of Omri. In 850 Ahab met his death fighting the Arameans at Ramoth-Gilead, across the Jordan (I Kings 22:35). He was succeeded by his son Ahaziah, who reigned only a few months, in 850/849, before he met his death as the result of a fall, (II Kings 1:17). He was succeeded by his brother Jehoram (849–842), who tried to modify his father's religious syncretism, although the continued presence of the queen mother precluded any real reform here (II Kings 3:2).

There were at least three forces ranged against the luckless Jehoram. There were the Yahweh prophets, now led by Elisha. There were conservative religious orders like the Rechabites, whose dress and ascetic habits called the people back to the old faith. There were elements of the army—a general was to become the leader of the revolt and the successor of Jehoram as king. The unfortunate Jehoram was in the family home at Jezreel recuperating from an accident when Elisha set the revolution in motion. The prophet sent an emissary to Ramoth-Gilead (still under contention) to anoint Jehu as the new king. Anti-Omride forces rallied to Jehu, who drove his chariot furiously toward Jezreel and Jehoram. He was met by

Jehoram and his visitor, King Ahaziah of Judah. Jehu killed them both. He then entered Jezreel, where he murdered Jezebel and what was left with her there of the Omride family. Jehu then moved to Samaria, where he found a delegation from the Jerusalem court. He murdered them too. Then he enticed all the functionaries of the baal religion into their temple, where he killed them all; then he burned the temple, with all its paraphernalia, to the ground (II Kings 9:1–10:31). "It was a purge of unspeakable brutality, beyond excuse from a moral point of view, which had . . . disastrous consequences. But the cult of Ba'al Melqart had been extirpated; Yahweh would remain, at least officially, the God of Israel."[14]

When the Israelite tribes moved into Palestine they carried their traditional faith, developed in the desert, into a hostile environment. The cult of Jezebel, the service of Baal Melqart, was one manifestation of a religion and culture that prevailed throughout the Fertile Crescent.[15] Because Jezebel was a zealous missionary for her god, she represented the gravest threat to the ancient faith of Israel. Yet that faith did survive, and Jezebel herself perished with her husband's dynasty. The opposition to her was incarnate in a prophet whose name, Elijah, means "Yahweh is my God" and whose memory was kept alive by stories which recounted his exploits for the old-time religion of Israel. Some of these stories told of his great public deeds, whereby he confronted Jezebel and Ahab and frustrated their plans for the extermination of Yahwism. Of these stories, the most dramatic told of his contest with the 450 prophets of Baal on Mount Carmel. Other stories represented the kind of pious anecdote that gathers around any great hero, prophet, or saint.

Some of these stories were selected and written down in a connected account, and to them were added stories about his successor Elisha and other prophets like Micaiah ben Imlah. When the great editor-writer whom we call the deuteronomic historian put together the long account of Isarel's history that begins with the death of Moses and ends with the destruction of Jerusalem he included, with other ancient sources, this collection of prophet stories about Elijah and Elisha and the others. For the most part he put this collection in as he found it. Because he regarded the reign of Ahab as very important, a moment of deep crisis and of victory for faith, he did not dismiss the period with the few words he expended on other kings, especially rulers of the northern kingdom, which he regarded as apostate in its very existence. He filled in the reign of Ahab with the Elijah stories and with fairly long accounts of Ahab's war with Damascus. His work became eventually part of the canon of Israel's scriptures, although not until long after both Israel and Judah had disappeared as independent nations. Perhaps six-hundred years

41

after his time, Elijah was immortalized in the scriptures of Judaism. Yet his role in history is secure. He emerges from story, cycle, history, and canon as a flesh-and-blood man whom we will now meet as he stands in the expropriated vineyard of the murdered Naboth.

3 IN THE VINEYARD OF NABOTH THE JEZREELITE

Having set the cycle of Elijah stories in its literary and historical context, we now turn to I Kings 21, the account of the judicial murder of the unfortunate Naboth. In the Hebrew Bible (and thus in our English translations) the Naboth story is set between the account of Ahab's victory over Benhadad of Damascus in chapter 20, and his last battle and death before Ramoth-Gilead which is told in chapter 22. Each of the two battle accounts is accompanied by a prophet-story. In 20:35-43 an unnamed prophet rebukes Ahab for sparing Benhadad contrary to the demands of the Holy War (Deut. 20:16-18; I Sam. 15:3); he announces Ahab's coming doom as judgment for this apostate leniency. The account of Ahab's final battle in chapter 22 is preceded by the story of Micaiah ben Imlah, a prophet who, in lonely contrast to his sychophantic colleagues, refuses to predict victory for Ahab and Jehoshaphat should they attack Ramoth-Gilead; instead Ahab will lose both the battle and his life (22:5-28). Elijah was not the only prophet of doom with whom poor Ahab had to cope! He goes to his death in the face of a three fold prophecy of doom from three different men of God:

"Your life shall go for his life, and your people for his people." (I Kings 20:42 RSV)

"In the place where dogs licked up the blood of Naboth shall dogs lick your own blood." (21:19 RSV)

"If you return in peace, the Lord has not spoken to me." (22:28 RSV)

The second of these predictions was not exactly fulfilled. Ahab does die, but the dogs lick up his blood not in Jezreel but in Samaria (22:38).[1]

Thus we see that in the Hebrew Bible the story of Naboth is detached from the Elijah cycle (17:1–19:21) and set in the midst of the war-diary

44

source. In the Greek Bible (the Septuagint) chapters 20 and 21 seem to be transposed. The Naboth story is chapter 20, and the victory over Benhadad is chapter 21. The Greek order may very well be older, for it keeps the Elijah-cycle and the war-diaries together, and apart from each other. The Greek may well depend on an earlier Hebrew text than the present Hebrew text, which shows an editorial decision to put the threefold prediction of Ahab's death immediately before that event.[2]

The Naboth story is quite unlike the other stories about Elijah. In fact the story is not really about Elijah at all, but about Naboth, Ahab, and Jezebel. The man of God is in no way involved in the action. He appears only after Naboth is disgraced, murdered, and his land expropriated. Elijah can do nothing about it. No wounds are healed, no wrongs are righted, no dead are raised. Elijah appears solely to announce the word of judgment upon Ahab and Jezebel. So this is far from an Elijah success story. It is found in the deuteronomic history, and thus in the Bible, because it shows that the judgments of history are predicted and brought to pass by the word of Yahweh uttered through the voice of his prophets. Ahab died at Ramoth-Gilead and Samaria because he deserved to die in that he ignored the exterminating demand of the Holy War (I Kings 20:42), and he killed a fellow Israelite and seized his land (I Kings 21:19), and he turned away from the counsel of a true prophet (I Kings 22:28). But he did not have to suffer the sight of the final purging of his dynasty because he did show remorse for his evil deeds (I Kings 21:27-29). This, say our editors, is the lesson of Ahab's sad reign.

The text of I Kings 21 can be translated as follows:

Naboth Refuses to Sell his Plot of Land to Ahab
(Vss. 1-7)

(1) Naboth the Jezreelite had a vineyard in his hometown near the residence of Ahab, the king of Samaria. (2) Ahab spoke thus to Naboth: "Would you please let me have your vineyard? It would make a garden for my estate here, for it is near my house. I will provide a better vineyard in exchange or, if you prefer, I will pay a fair amount of cash for it." (3) But Naboth said to Ahab: "It would be a profane, ungodly thing for me to turn my vineyard over to you, for it is a sacred paternal inheritance." (4) So Ahab went home, sullen and angry, because this local Naboth had rejected his offer. He threw himself down on his bed, turned his face to the wall, and refused to eat anything. (5) When his wife Jezebel came to him she said, "What is the meaning of this sulking and fasting?" (6) So he told her, "I spoke to this local Naboth fellow and I offered him money, or if he preferred, another vineyard for his piece of land,

and he flatly refused my offer." (7) Jezebel his wife said to him, "You really are acting like a mere Israelite king! Get up, eat, cheer up, be a man—I will see that you get the vineyard of Naboth the Jezreelite."

How Jezebel Got the Vineyard for Ahab
(Vss. 8-16)

(8) So she drew up a document, to which she affixed Ahab's signature and royal seal, and sent it to the elders and influential men, Naboth's neighbors, and fellow-citizens. (9) She had the document say:

Proclaim a fast!

Make Naboth sit at the head of the local assembly.

(10) Then set up two thugs opposite him and let them accuse him under oath: "You have cursed God and the king." Then take him outside and stone him to death.

(11) Naboth's fellow-citizens—elders and influential men, acted exactly as Jezebel had requested in this document addressed to them. (12) They proclaimed a fast and set Naboth up at the head of the local assembly. (13) And they produced the two thugs who sat opposite him and solemnly accused him, saying: "Naboth has cursed God and the king." So they took him out beyond the town limits where they stoned him until he

47

died. (14) Then they reported to Jezebel that Naboth had been stoned and was dead. (15) When Jezebel heard this she notified Ahab: "Get up, take possession of the vineyard which Naboth the Jezreelite refused to sell you, for Naboth is no longer alive—he is dead." (16) When Ahab learned of Naboth's death he got up and went down to the vineyard of Naboth the Jezreelite to expropriate it.

The Judgment of Yahweh, by the Hand of Elijah
(Vss. 17-20a, 23)

(17) The word of Yahweh came unto Elijah the Tishbite saying: (18) "Get up, go down to meet Ahab, the king of Israel who rules from Samaria; for, see, he is in Naboth's vineyard which he has gone down to expropriate. (19) You shall deliver this divine oracle:

So, you have murdered and expropriated!
This, therefore, is Yahweh's oracle:
In the place where the dogs licked Naboth's blood,
There the dogs will lick your blood—yours too!

(20) And Ahab said to Elijah: "Have you found me, my enemy?" And he said: "Yes, I have. . . ." (23) Yahweh also had an oracle directed to Jezebel, thus:

The dogs will eat Jezebel within the territory of Jezreel.

Three Editorial Comments on the Story of Naboth's Vineyard

Editor A: (20b-22, 24)

(20b) ". . . because you have sold yourself to do evil in Yahweh's eyes, (21) look, I am bringing calamity upon you. I will totally consume what you leave behind, and I will cut off from Ahab every male, slave or free man, in Israel, (22) and I will make your house like the house of Jeroboam the son of Nebat, and like the house of Baasha the son of Ahijah, for you have provoked me to great anger—you have caused Israel to sin. . . . (24) The dogs shall eat Ahab's men who die in the city, and the birds of the air will eat those who die in the open country."

Editor B: Probably the Deuteronomic Historian (25, 26)

(25) Never was there anyone like Ahab who sold himself to do the evil thing in the eyes of Yahweh, because Jezebel his wife inflamed him. (26) He disgracefully went after the idols just like the Amorites, whom Yahweh had dispossessed in favor of the Israelites.

Editor C: Written to Harmonize 21:19 with 22:37, 38 (27-29)

(27) Now it happened, as Ahab heard these words, he tore his clothing and put sackcloth on his body and fasted, and lay down in sackcloth and

went about in sad despair. (28) So the word of Yahweh came unto Elijah the Tishbite saying (29) "Have you seen how subdued Ahab is before me? Therefore I will not bring the calamity in his time. In the time of his son I will bring the calamity upon his house."

Running Commentary on I Kings 21

Verse 1: The Hebrew text of I Kings 21:1 reads: "And it came to pass after these events, there was a vineyard belonging to Naboth the Jezreelite which was in Jezreel near the residence of Ahab, the king of Samaria." The first clause is editorial, joining the story of Naboth to the war chronicle which precedes it; it is omitted in one of the Greek manuscripts. The expression "which was in Jezreel" is missing in nearly all the main Greek manuscripts. It seems to be unnecessarily repetitive; its probable intention is to stress that the events about to be described occurred in Jezreel, not in Samaria. Indeed the events in chapter 21 almost certainly did take place in Jezreel, a town on the plain of Esdraelon (this name is the Greek form of "Jezreel") about twenty miles north-north-east of Samaria. Very likely, Jezreel was the family home of the Omrides. In I Kings 18:46 Ahab returns from Mount Carmel to Jezreel. In II Kings 8:29 and 9:15 we find Joram, the son of Ahab, convalescing in Jezreel. Jezebel, the queen mother after the death of Ahab, lives in Jezreel where she meets her own hideous death (II Kings 9:30-37) as do Joram (II Kings 9:21-26) and the residue of the house of Ahab (II Kings 10:11). It would appear that the family home of the Omrides was Jezreel and that they still regarded this town as their own rather than the still incomplete Samaria from which they ruled.[3]

Only in this verse and in II Kings 1:3 is the Israelite king designated as "king of Samaria," although he is sometimes so styled in the Assyrian records. The use of the term here in the Elijah cycle may indicate some editor's contempt for the claim of the Omrides to be kings of Israel.[4]

Verses 2 and 3: Ahab makes a fair offer to Naboth—a better piece of land or a cash settlement. Naboth's refusal is based on the religious conviction that land is to be held within the family as a sacred stewardship. It is held in trust for Yahweh. An ancient Hebrew law code, the Holiness Code (Leviticus 19–26), deals with land holding, especially in chapter 25. If an Israelite freeman becomes so impoverished that he has to sell his land, and he subsequently cannot raise the money to redeem it, it must still be returned to him or his heirs in the year of jubilee (Lev. 25:28).[5]

In Jeremiah 32:1-44 we see the prophet buying a field in Anatoth, his hometown, because, as the next-of-kin to the man who must sell it, Jeremiah is entitled to buy it. He does this, although the area is under siege and he himself has said that it will fall to the Chaldeans. But not even the fall of Jerusalem and Judah will deprive the Israelite freeman of his land, for the land belongs to Yahweh and those who hold it in trust from him and for him. Naboth's refusal to sell his property, then, derives from a firm religious conviction, and Ahab is still enough of a member of the believing community to understand this refusal. He does not believe that he can do anything about it, despite his bitter disappointment.

Verse 4: The literal translation of the Hebrew is as follows: "And Ahab came into his house, sullen and angry, on account of the word which Naboth the Jezreelite spoke to him when he said, 'I will not give you the inheritance of my fathers, and he lay down upon his couch, and turned his face in, and did not eat bread." The Greek translation is shorter, and reads: "And the spirit of Ahab was vexed, and he lay down upon his bed, and covered his face, and ate no bread. . . ." The Latin Vulgate, presumably resting here on another text reads, "And he turned his face to the wall. . . ." This is the way King Hezekiah is said to have reacted in a similar situation (II Kings 20:2). These variants in verse 4 are a good example of the kind of differences that abound in our texts. The standard text here has been expanded from several shorter versions. They all add up to a disappointed and frustrated Ahab who is found sulking by his wife.

Verses 5-7 describe her reaction to Ahab's depression. Her word to him recorded in verse 7 is capable of different shades of meaning which depend on the tone of voice. Literally the Hebrew text reads: "You now are exercising kingship over Israel." The Greek text makes it a question: "Is this the way a king of Israel acts?" Jezebel simply cannot understand a political situation in which the ruler cannot get what he wants when he wants it. Only an *Israelite* king would be so chicken-hearted. But this kind of inhibition on royal power, this form of limited monarchy, was always characteristic of Israel. Why should David not have Uriah's wife, or Ahab not have Naboth's vineyard? Jezebel has nothing but scorn for the kind of power that allows a ruler to be frustrated in his covetousness by a mere subject. "Why can't you act like a real king? If you can't, I will," she says in effect.

Verses 8-16: Her evil deed is recounted. She forges the king's signature and uses his royal seal on documents proclaiming a fast. A fast was an act of community repentance in an emergency situation. A present peril must be due to some hidden fault (Joel 1:14; Jon. 3:7-9, where an Assyrian king acts like an Israelite!). In I Samuel 7:6 Saul proclaims just such an emergency-induced fast; the peril here is the Philistine threat.

Naboth is set at the head of the people. Was that his natural place because he was the "mayor" —the first citizen—or was he put there because that is the seat of the accused? We are not sure. Jezebel is scrupulous about the formalities of Israelite law which require accusation from the mouth of two witnesses who agree (Deut. 17: 6-7, 19: 15, reflected in Matt. 26: 60). Jezebel has to raise her witnesses from the disreputable elements in the community. Probably because the populace feared her, this kind of accusation was sufficient to convict the unfortunate Naboth of cursing God and the king. The Hebrew text actually reads: "You blessed God and the king." But this is a scribal correction for the original "cursed"; the correction was made to protect the reader from uttering the words "curse" and "God" together and thus becoming himself involved in blasphemy! Leviticus 24: 16 indicated that the penalty for blasphemy is stoning by the whole community. It is interesting to note that the same law code (Lev. 19–26) is the authority for Naboth's refusal to give up his land; it is also the law under which he is condemned to die. This part of the Pentateuch seems certainly to have been in effect in the northern kingdom of the ninth century. In a later notice of this sad event, Naboth's family is executed with him (II Kings 9: 26) in his own field (II Kings 9: 25).

With Naboth dead, Ahab goes down to the

vineyard to possess it. The suggestion has been made that he was a relative of Naboth and had the right of inheritance after Naboth and his family.[6] More likely he simply exercised a royal power on confiscation. In any case, he goes down to Naboth's vineyard, where Yahweh sends Elijah to meet him.

*Verses 17-20*a give an account of the confrontation between Ahab and the man of God. Verse 18 reads, literally: "Arise, go down to meet Ahab the king of Israel, who is in Samaria; behold, he is in the vineyard of Naboth, where he has gone to take possession" (RSV). It has been suggested that throughout this chapter and in II Kings 1:3 "Samaria" is a gloss; in 21:18 the glossarist is one who believed that Naboth, though a Jezreelite, had his land next to the royal palace in Samaria.[7] It is perhaps more likely that here the use of the term "in Samaria" betrays an attitude of contempt toward the Omride dynasty and its new capital: "the king of Israel, who rules from Samaria"—that self-styled king and his new capital! There is really little doubt that the action throughout chapter 21 takes place in Jezreel, the home of Naboth and almost as certainly the family home of the house of Omri.

In verse 19 we have a simple prophetic oracle in three parts:

a) the reason for the judgment—"so you have murdered and expropriated . . ."

b) the authority for the judgment—"therefore thus says Yahweh . . ."

c) the sentence—"in the place where the dogs licked Naboth's blood there the dogs will lick your blood—yours too!"

In our discussion of verses 27-29 we will have to look at the fact that this sentence was not precisely fulfilled in the case of Ahab for he was mortally wounded in battle before Ramoth-Gilead (22:34) and went to Samaria to die, and it was there that the dogs licked his blood as it dripped from his chariot and the harlots washed themselves in it (22:37-38).

We accept the dialogue between Elijah and Ahab that follows this pronouncement ("Have you found me, my enemy. . . . Yes, I have"—21:20), and also verse 23, Yahweh's sentence of judgment on Jezebel: "The dogs will eat Jezebel within the territory of Jezebel, as part of the early prophetic narrative. There are some authorities who take verse 23 as prophecy after the event—the event being Jezebel's assassination at the hands of Jehu and his holy thugs (II Kings 9:30-37).[8] But there is no real reason to take these words away from Elijah. It seems reasonable that Jezebel, the real antagonist, would be included in the judgmental sentence and that it would not even require prophetic insight to predict that her death would occur in Jezreel, the Omride family home.

But the rest of the material in this chapter almost certainly consists of editorial comment. The words in verses 21 and 22 re-echo the very words of the prophet Ahijah pronouncing doom upon Jeroboam I in I Kings 14:10 and the words of a prophet called Jehu in 16:3 pronouncing his doom on Baasha, another of Ahab's unhappy predecessors. They may be the words of the editor of a document consisting of stories of the prophets into which the Elijah saga cycle has been phased. This document would be one of the sources of the Kings books,[9] used by the deuteronomic historian and editor whose own judgment on Ahab is given in verses 25 and 26.

The other editorial addition (vss. 27-29) is more interesting. The judgment of Elijah on Ahab given in verse 19 was not precisely and literally fulfilled in the manner of his death, for he actually died honorably as the result of wounds suffered in battle. Part of the judgment of 21:19, then, is deferred to the obliteration of Ahab's dynasty, which occurred when his son Joram was murdered by Jehu and his body was thrown on the site of Naboth's vineyard (II Kings 9:21-26). Thus Elijah's judgment was realized in two stages: (1) Ahab was killed in battle, and the dogs licked his blood; (2) his line was wiped out in Jezreel, on this very plot of ground.

To call these later verses in chapter 21 "editorial comments" or "redactional" is not the same thing as saying that they are fictional, or worthless, or no part of scripture, or nonhistorical. There is nothing inherently improbable in the report of the repentance of Ahab. Throughout his career he was depicted as "incited" by Jezebel. His reluctance to expropriate Naboth's vineyard showed his regard for the holy traditions and laws of Israel. The fact may well be that Ahab did repent, a later interpreter seeing in his being granted an honorable death the reward for that repentance. The God of Israel does change his mind at times; there is always the hope that in the face of a sincere "returning" on the part of his people, or indeed of aliens (Jon. 3:10), he himself may "repent" and soften threatened judgments.

The three editorial additions could be regarded as early "sermons" on the life of Ahab and the Naboth incident. The first preacher (20b-22, 24) expanded on the wickedness of Ahab and saw that this wickedness brought about the ruin and end of his dynasty. The second (25:26) simply stated that Ahab was the most wicked of all, and attributed this evil to the incitement of his wife. The third (27-29) reflected on Ahab's honorable death and saw in this apparent nonfulfillment of Elijah's prediction the fruit of Ahab's repentance.[10]

4 how to get lost in naboth's vineyard, and how to begin to find your way through

Lakeport is a city of several hundred thousand located on the shore of one of the lower Great Lakes. For our purpose it does not matter whether it is located in New York, Pennsylvania, Ohio, or across the water and the international boundary in Ontario. In many ways it is a depressing place in which to live and an impossible place to govern. It has all the faults of its innumerable sister cities. The inner hub is an area of decay, and from it the spokes of urban sprawl radiate and grow as if they were a luxuriant species of vine. No perimeter rim or green belt stops them. The city spews its sewage into its poisoned lake. It is aware that it is thus destroying itself, turning off the water that gives it life. But it cannot raise the money to stop this. With the help of senior governments on both sides of the lake it hopes to do so some day. Its educational institutions, particularly its secondary schools, are too numerous, big, and elaborate for the age of "the Pill" and a declining population. Education is by now almost prohibitively expensive, financed by personal property tax, and so educational expenditures are now increasingly resented. Above it all the towers of the high-rise culture rear their similar and square heads. For there is now no place to go but up. The entrepreneurs who see this situation and cash in on it are called "developers." They are heroes to the older, traditional municipal politicians, for their products represent a renewed tax base. But they are villains to a new breed of local leaders who see their buildings as tombs and sepulchres for the spirit of man.

Lakeport has too many churches. Some of them, built in the late fifties, are new and shiny, resplendent with glass and as full of gadgets as a fruitcake is full of nuts. One of these is Hynes Heights Denominational Church, located out toward the end of one of the city's spokes. It is an area where a university campus once stood in the country, but the city reached out toward the campus in its growth. In the mid-sixties the church added an "educational plant." This was done before the later theological fads of that fanciful decade made excrescences of such extravagances. Right now you cannot walk through the place without tripping over, or being in danger of strangulation by, the electrical gear of the communications media. The pastor and his staff always say "media" when they mean "medium," they say "input" when they mean speech or sermon, they say "task force" when they mean committee, and they are almost old-fashioned enough to say "I will contact him" when they mean they will telephone or write him.

The present senior minister, the Reverend Jeremy Brown, is not really very senior, but he likes the title, although he often hastens to say that his colleagues—the Minister of Education, the Minister of Music and the elderly Minister of Visitation—are part of the "collegium." Jeremy is an educational product of the turbulent sixties. He went to a rather small and discreet college of his denomination, so missed most of the yeastier ferment of that memorable time. But he considered himself moderately radical, a follower of Cox and Shaull, rather than Altizer and Hamilton. He identified himself as a social activist early in his seminary career. The seminary he attended was in a cluster of which his denominational college

was one of the larger and more luscious grapes.
Jeremy Brown is sincere in his social concern. As
a seminarian he spent endless hours in ghetto
coffee shops, and once made the obligatory pil-
grimage south on a freedom march. The closest
he ever came to the counterculture was a sur-
reptitious puff or two on a joint. It did not turn
him on. If pressed, Jeremy would be honest enough
to admit that he did not really dig youth music.
He never joined the Woodstock Nation. He was
never in jail. And because early in his seminary
career he met and married a sensitive and
beautiful girl whose openness never quite included
the freedom of the more spectacular communes or
the more picturesque aspects of women's liberation, Jeremy became somewhat career oriented
before he graduated, one of the earlier Masters of
Divinity who now replaced the rather sad and
faded Bachelors of the preceding era.

Early upward mobility has characterized
Jeremy's short career in the ministry. After two
short years as Minister of Education, with oc-
casional preaching responsibilities, in a very large
church, he became senior minister at Hynes
Heights. He was not yet thirty years old and the
very recent happy father of a daughter, whom
he called Jennifer. The call to Hynes Heights for
Jeremy caused a lot of head-shaking among his
elders in less conspicuous positions, who predicted
that the fruit of his immaturity would be a short,

disastrous, and unhappy pastorate. Busy with their own innumerable concerns—business, family, and tribal—the rising young executives and their families who inhabit Hynes Heights pay little attention to the opinions and habits of their ministers. Jeremy, as befits a liberated type, smoked his pipe openly and became almost a connoisseur of good California and New York wines. Not much more was required of him than that, under his direction, the church provide some instruction and activity for the children and younger teen-agers as well as tasteful worship services, which the parishioners attended rather faithfully when the weather was neither too fair nor too foul.

Each Labor Day Jeremy preached an activist sermon. It could safely be fairly radical because, on that Sunday, church was rather peripheral in the concerns of most Hynes Heighters. They had to close the cottage and get the kids ready for school. The few who did turn up were from the more radical element who kept off the roads on Labor Day weekend as a protest against pollution and traffic jams—actually they had their own swimming pools and air-conditioned homes and patios which they sensibly preferred to the throughway; they deferred their holidays to the winter when they went skiing in Vermont or Quebec, or perhaps scuba diving in Antigua. For the annual Labor Day sermon (also for the Festival of the Christian Family and Reformation Sunday)

63

Jeremy consulted a book called *Sermon Starters from Scripture,* which he kept concealed behind more respectable tomes such as a four-volume commentary on the Bible. One of the texts suggested under "Action, social" was I Kings 21. This is how Jeremy Brown found his way into Naboth's vineyard on Labor Day Sunday, 197X.

To the 111 gathered (average for September; augmented by a special effort on the third Sunday called "Back to Church and School" Sunday there would be 193) the Reverend Jeremy Brown spoke feelingly about the Naboths, the exploited in our society. He was concerned for minority groups, for pensioners caught in the inflationary spiral, for those working long hours in the service industries which cater to the rich, for lettuce pickers safely remote in California. He was balanced enough to see that modern unionism had some of the same temptations to exploitation and manipulation as modern multinational corporations. But the latter were the big villains. They exploit the poor in South Africa, South America, and other places closer to home. He saw in the coming winter, with its possible fossil fuel shortage, a judgment on all of us rich Ahabs for the lack of concern and stewardship which we display when we spend our God-given riches on ourselves. This winter, Jezebel may still live in an ivory palace, but it will be a cold ivory palace, and Ahab's chariot may sit silent in the stable for lack of "horses." Naboth represents all who are the casualties of "man's inhumanity to man."

Hynes Heights Denominational Church was actually a spin-off from First Denominational in downtown Lakeport. That is the way Jeremy Brown says it. Old First itself uses the more sedate term "mother church," and she has mothered four others besides Hynes Heights; three of her children are living and breathing. One was stillborn, and another died of ecumenical amalgamation. Old First looks a bit like a nineteenth-century bank. It has the same four columns and the same break-into-me-if-you-can challenging appearance. This is natural enough, as bankers were prominent among the founders of Old First a century or so ago. The minister at Old First now is George Victor Smythe. He is a little older than Jeremy Brown, having well begun a career in certified accounting before training for the ministry. He is thus of the same student generation, but he took another course, discovering the Young Americans for Freedom in his college days. His heroes, along with Adam Smith and Edmund Burke, are the Buckley brothers and some University of Chicago economists, whose names he cannot remember and whose books he cannot understand. George Victor was a little older than his fellow seminarians, and his conservatism and celibacy made him seem a little odd to them. But he was never very militant.

He looked upon such popular heroes of the right as Vice-President Agnew and Governor Reagan in rather the same way as he regarded Billy Graham and Liberace—maybe necessary for the masses. The reading he likes best is John Henry Newman's *Plain and Parochial Sermons,* and sometimes in the night watches he entertains the idea that the only logical way for a true conservative is the way found at last by the Cardinal. As George Victor Smythe is still a bachelor, this way is still an option for him.

His sparse congregation drives a long way, some of them right past Hynes Heights, to keep Old First in business at the old stand. When they do arrive they are treated to a minimum of liturgy and a closely reasoned lecture which sees a clear and obvious connection between the freedom of the marketplace and the other freedoms. The rather prosaic freedom of the businessman to make money could not be eroded away without undermining also the four freedoms—freedom of speech, of religion, of the press—and even freedom from want. For are not the poor of the capitalist world rich beyond the imagination of the masses in Cuba and China? Smythe's parishioners, themselves mostly businessmen and their families, think this is all slightly odd coming from the pulpit. They rather expect to be pilloried a bit (not too seriously!) from that rostrum. To be assured that in making money they are serving God and man makes them feel a little uneasy. For some obscure reason they do not find this support comforting, and Mr. Smythe is not particularly popular with them.

It is almost impossible to visit the scattered congregation of Old First, so George Victor does a lot of reading. One day he came across a sermon preached by Monsignor Ronald Knox in his late Anglican days. The sermon is called "Naboth's Vineyard in Pawn." In it Knox likens the seizure of monasteries and other church properties by Henry VIII to Ahab's seizure of Naboth's vineyard.[1] Smythe easily translated this into the modern scene and saw in the "galloping" (he had abandoned "creeping") socialism and welfarism of modern democratic society the state (Ahab) taking more and more and leaving less and less room for man (Naboth) to move around in and to be free. Fabianism and even the New Deal are the soft words of Ahab ("I will give you another and a better vineyard. . . . I will pay you fair compensation"); Castro and Allende are the hard deeds of Jezebel. This posed a bit of an exegetical problem for George Victor Smythe, who is no fool. For Naboth had indeed resisted the soft words of Ahab, and this resistance did not really prepare him for the iron deeds of Jezebel. But you cannot make a parable stand on all four legs, and Smythe figured (correctly) that his congregation would not notice this bit of inconsistency. He was carried

67

away by his favorite rhetoric before he had set foot very far into the vineyard of Naboth the Jezreelite.

Second Denominational is not one of Old First's daughters. This church is located not far from Old First and owes its origin to the conviction of the denomination's fathers that both the Calvinist (First) and Arminian (Second) palate had to be catered to in Lakeport. Nobody around Second today, including the pastor, could tell an Arminian from an apricot. In fact it is doubtful if the fine theological distinction that gave it birth was ever appreciated by the members of Second. They tend to come from a less elevated socioeconomic stratum than do the members of First or Hynes Heights. If I were permitted to say it in English, I would say that most of them were and are poor people, and the members of both First and the Heights were and are, for the most part, rich people. Old First-ers have always tended to be a bit patronizing about Seconders and have always taken a rather tolerantly dim view of the fact that Second almost always has had more people in church and Sunday School and has raised more money for missions. By the time of World War II, however, it appeared that Second Denominational Church had had it. The methodist enthusiasm of its youth had faded, and even the institutional revival of the fifties did not reach it. Its renewal as a force in Lakeport came when the Reverend W. Bennett Bracey accepted its call in 1960. Since then, as Ben would say, "Statisticswise we're being blessed of the Lord."

One of Ben's slogans is: "Everything Modern but the Gospel." His congregation (he likes to say "constituency") was certainly new to Second. Some of the old Second families has succeeded in moving out to Hynes Heights and other suburbs, and others, unable to cope with Ben, went over to First or drifted away altogether. But the Sunday school bussing, and the advertising campaign which Ben instituted, certainly much more than replaced them with new people. You cannot get on a city bus in Lakeport without seeing there, among the advertising cards for Creme Shampoo and Canadian Club whisky, a message from Ben Bracey and Second Denominational Church.

> Bible Believing
> Christ Centered
> Air Conditioned

is one of the quieter cards. Dr. Ben Bracey (he had picked up his honorary degree somewhere since coming in 1960) had indeed changed the church, including the physical plant and the equipment. Theater chairs had replaced uncomfortable pews, groups of singers and instrumentalists had replaced choirs, a well-lighted and equipped kindergarten facility had replaced the gloomy Sheol that was

69

the scene of Christmas entertainments in antiquity. But Dr. Bracey did not bring in a public address system. He believed that to be kept on his homiletical toes he must always face the challenge of geriatric hearing disabilities and rise a few decibels above it.

Bracey is actually quite a bit older than either Brown or Smythe but he thinks that he looks younger, and perhaps he does. At the moment the popular cause that he is attacking most enthusiastically is women's liberation. His wife, who is celebrated by her lord as right out of Proverbs 31: 10-31, cooperates happily in this scenario. The Braceys have four children—two in a "Christian college" in Georgia, one in high school (a boy, with the only crew cut left in grade X), and a little girl who is very beautiful and rightfully spoiled as she tears around the church building.

Although the historic Christian year would have no attraction for Dr. Ben if he ever heard of it, he has his own church year. Each Sunday is potentially high (good prospects for a crowd) or low (problem Sundays). One of the problem Sundays is the third Sunday in May. The second Sunday, Mother's Day, is as "high" as Easter or Rally Day. But in the climate of Lakeport the third Sunday in May is very likely to be such (and the first such) as to tempt the tepid worshiper with the notion that the church year is phasing out and summer is icumen in.

For lo, the winter is past,
  the rain is over and gone,
the flowers appear on the earth,
  the time of the singing of birds has come
and the voice of the outboard engine is heard
  on our lakes.

Dr. Ben met the low Sundays with special advertising, instrumental and vocal groups of proved virtuosity and fame, and a particularly arresting sermon title. He increased the size of his Saturday church-page ad and usually managed to get himself invited on one of the morning radio talk shows, where he discussed the acutely topical theme for the coming low Sunday. This year the theme for MD + 1 was "Women's Liberation and the Word of God," and his text was the word of Jezebel to her husband in I Kings 21:7: "I will give you the vineyard of Naboth the Jezreelite." If Ahab had enjoyed the counsel of the Apostle Paul (Eph. 5:23), or for that matter of Dr. Ben Bracey, he would have stood by his first instinct, which was based on the Word of God, and let Naboth keep his vineyard. For the Word of God, in Deut. 5:21 says: "You shall not covet your neighbor's field"—among other things. The Word of God in Ps. 45:11 tells the woman, even when she is a queen, what her place is: "Since he is your lord, bow to him." The Word of God in Gen. 3:17—the very first word spoken by God to man as a male!—says: "Because you listened

71

to the voice of your wife . . . I will curse the ground on your behalf . . ."

In These Last Days women stand in great danger. This is one of the signs of the times and the end of the age (II Tim. 3:6). Let them flee to the authority of the Word of God, and hence to the protecting arms of their husbands. Let them be like Rahab the harlot and seek the protection of the scarlet cord in the window (Josh. 2:18), which is the shed blood of Jesus. If they do this they will be saved in the day of tribulation. For Rahab was spared in the day of Jericho's fall to doom. The city was destroyed never to be rebuilt, but Rahab and her family were saved, though as by fire (I Cor. 3:15). Jezebel, on the other hand, although she had a more respectable occupation (a queen has some kind of edge on a whore), was untrue to the best interests of her earthly lord and deaf to the Word of the heavenly Lord, so she was killed by the Lord's avenger Jehu, whose name (Dr. Ben looked this up somewhere) means "He is Jehovah." Her flesh was eaten up on the streets of Jezreel by the dogs. This theme was enlivened with contemporary allusions and illustrations in which several notorious women's lib protagonists were compared, somewhat unfavorably, to Jezebel. The sermon was indeed eloquent and was enjoyed by the 654 present, especially the 476 women. Twenty-four responded to the invitation, 21 of them girls and women. On the whole, MD + 1 compared very favorably to MD itself. On MD there were, it is true, 812 present, but only 13 responded to the invitation.

These word portraits are, of course, caricatures. But I would argue that the use of Scripture made by Brown, Smythe, and Bracey not unfairly represents the kind of textual and expository preaching that happens all too often. Each of these preachers takes his vision of life and faith *to* the Scripture. He comes to the Bible with his answers —answers which are formed by his own experience—his education, convictions, prejudices, presuppositions. We do not contend that these answers are altogether false. We can stand with Jeremy Brown and proclaim that biblical faith sees God on the side of the poor and exploited; with George Victor Smythe we can be sensitive to the danger to freedom inherent in power, including the power of the democratic state—a danger that may persist even when good is intended. With Dr. Bennett Bracey we can contend that men and women are indeed sinners who stand in need of the remedy whose cost to God is symbolized in the shed blood of his only begotten Son. The problem with each of these interpreters is that he takes his answer to the Bible seeking texts that will confirm and illustrate and dramatize it. If we listen for the Word of God in Scripture we may hear something new or, what is most

73

fearful, new to us; it will perhaps bring the light of judgment on the dark places of our own life and set of opinions. He who would proclaim the Word must be addressed himself by the Word. And there is no "devotional" or incidental reading that can abridge the serious study of Scripture.

So the road into Naboth's vineyard is a long road, and there are no short cuts. The reader may come to I Kings 21 because he is following a lectionary, or doing a systematic reading of the Old Testament or a special study on the theme "prophecy." He brings to this text questions to which he seeks answers, not answers for which he expects confirmation and illustration. In the following pages I shall suggest seven questions to bring to a biblical passage. If we can answer these questions we will understand the text, and then, and only then, will we be able to share our understanding with those to whom we minister through preaching and teaching.

1. What Is the Context of This Passage in Scripture?

The story of Naboth's vineyard is part of the Elijah saga-cycle, although this particular incident does not present the prophet in a heroic, saga-like role. The Elijah stories were very likely part of a larger source—stories of the early prophets

—and this source was used by the writers and collectors of I and II Kings. The prophetic source was not inserted as a whole, but broken up and the appropriate part inserted into the data which the editors had about each king. It would appear that the framework used was royal annals called "the chronicles of the kings of Judah" and "the chronicles of the kings of Israel" (I Kings 14:19, 29, etc.). The Elijah stories are found in the records of the reign of Ahab and his two sons in the northern kingdom. The material in I Kings 21 was placed immediately before the record of Ahab's last battle (I Kings 22). There is some evidence that this order was not the original, but was deliberately arranged to show exactly how the evil deeds of Ahab brought about his downfall and that of his dynasty.

The two books of Kings are part of a vast historical work which scholars have called the deuteronomic history. This work describes the history of Israel from the death of Moses (Jos. 1:1) to the fall of Jerusalem and the exile of Judah (II Kings 25:30). The account, using older sources (royal annals, war diaries, stories of the prophets, etc.) is edited and shaped to illustrate the historian's theological conviction that Israel prospered and had peace when faithful to her covenant with Yahweh, and suffered calamity and defeat when she turned to idolatry. Both kingdoms were incurably apostate, and the end of them was predetermined by their persistent unbelief and idolatry. This long account came to be part of the canon of the Hebrew Bible, where it is called "The Former Prophets." The whole work is prophecy in the sense of showing how history illustrates and illumines the way the word of God works in the affairs of men.

2. What Is the Historical Background of This Passage?

Elijah appeared in the ninth century B.C. in the reign of Ahab of Israel (the northern kingdom), who, incited by his pagan wife, Jezebel, was the most apostate of all the apostate northern kings. In this reign the eternal contest between Yahweh and the gods of Canaan (baalim) saw its moment of greatest crisis—the ancient faith of Israel was almost exterminated. The religions of Canaan involved idolatry, obscene (for the Hebrews) rites, and a system in which the traditional freedoms of the Hebrew citizen (including his right to live on his own land in his own person and in the person of his descendants) were seriously jeopardized. Both religious purity and social justice (these are inseparable in Hebrew thought) were threatened by the baalim and particularly by the Tyrian baal Melkart, whose champion was Jezebel. Elijah's judgment on Ahab and his descendants was fulfilled in the *coup d'état* of Jehu, who wiped out the dynasty of Ahab in the day of his son Joram.

3. What Are the Boundaries of the Passage?

. Biblical preaching is often divided into two types, textual and expository. In the first the preacher uses a verse of the Bible as the authority for his sermon; in the second he seeks to explain the meaning of a longer passage, perhaps a chapter. But the speakers and writers who gave us the Bible did not speak and write in verses and chapters. These divisions were imposed late upon Scripture as liturgical aids; they do not always correspond to natural thought units and sequences. One of the great values of form criticism for teaching and preaching is that this discipline helps us identify a literary unit, set its boundaries, and place it in its own setting in life. When, to whom, and for what reason was this prophetic oracle or gospel parable spoken, this law promulgated, this hymn sung? When and for what reason was it incorporated into the literature where we find it?

There are at least three units in I Kings 21. Verses 1-16 tell the story of the unhappy Naboth and his fate at the hands of Jezebel. Verses 17-20a and 23 tell of the confrontation between Elijah and Ahab. The rest of the chapter contains three (or more) commentaries or sermons on this incident and on the reign of Ahab. Undoubtedly the

77

story is preserved because of the prophetic confrontation. It is included in the Elijah stories although it is not primarily about Elijah. The story is placed in our Bible before the fatal events of I Kings 22—it is a dagger pointed at the heart of Ahab and his family.

4. Exactly What Does the Text Say?

When we have "rightly divided" our passage and chosen from it the portion that seems to carry its message, we face the question of the words themselves. What are the true words of the text, and what do they mean? We are now involved in textual criticism, translation, and word-study. The interpreter who is innocent of the biblical languages is dependent upon translations and commentaries. If he is to be a serious commentator himself he must find out what the best commentaries are and obtain them even if he has to sell his shirt. For I and II Kings there are two excellent commentaries in English—I have used them both extensively for this study. They are the *International Critical Commentary* on the books of Kings (Montgomery and Gehman) and John Gray's work on I and II Kings[2] For almost every part of the Bible there are superior commentaries. The serious Bible student can find out what they are through reviews in journals, or he can ask his own teachers. In chapter 3 of this study I sought to set forth, insofar as I could, the true text of I Kings 21.

5. What Theological Motifs Underlie This Passage?

In his important book *The Authority of the Old Testament,* John Bright contends that behind every text in the Old Testament there is an underlying theological conviction. This is true even of such apparently barren tracts as genealogies and obscure legal codes. This theological conviction is expressed in three motifs. One or more of these is found behind all texts: (1) the election of Israel, (2) the Lordship of Yahweh, (3) hope for the future for the people of God.[3]

Certainly in our passage the prominent motif is the Lordship of Yahweh. It is he, not Ahab or Jezebel or even Elijah, who will determine the final outcome of the action. The election theme is implied, and any hope for the future is dependent upon the end of the Omride dynasty. But this is not a passage we would normally turn to as a basis for the consideration of the theme of election or eschatology.

6. What Did the Original Hearers or Readers Understand by This Passage?

What does this narrative tell us about politics in ancient Israel? Were there some limits on the power of the state (king)? How did this differ from what went on in other nations? Does the story imply anything about the inherent right of Israelite citizens? By what authority does the prophet confront the king? Why does the king have to listen to him? What is the nature of the first editorial comments on this story? What lessons were apparent to those who gave us these supplements?

I Kings 21 yields the following kinds of answers to these questions. In ancient Israel there was a presumption that the freeman had certain inherent rights that the state (king) could not abrogate. Among these rights was the right of a family to hold land. Political power was not absolute. That the king was himself conscious of these limitations on his power, and somewhat inhibited by this knowledge, is seen twice—in his reluctance to expropriate in the face of Naboth's refusal to sell, and in his tolerance of the prophetic judgment and repentance before it. There seems to be in the prophetic role an inherent charismatic authority which the king recognized and respected. The role and act of Jezebel shows us that this kind of limitation did not obtain elsewhere, for she is used to raw political power and derides Ahab's reluctance to exercise it. Elsewhere in records about Jezebel we learn that, in her kind of court, prophets and priests exist to serve the ruler.

The first commentators saw in this event another evidence of Ahab's hopeless apostasy, which they attributed to Jezebel's influence. Another saw in his honorable death evidence that Yahweh softened his judgment in the face of Ahab's remorse.

7. What Does This Passage Say to Us Today in the Church?

The first personal plural pronoun and the word "church" are important. The Bible is not the place to look for private enlightenment. The Hebrew-Christian religion is historic and corporate. Salvation is not the soul's escape from society and history. It is a personal event—it can happen to me—but it happens to me as a person among persons, human and divine. Outside the church (Israel) there is indeed no salvation. It is not "well with my soul" if it is ill with the soul or body of my sister or brother.

The word "today" in this question is also important. There is material in the Bible, perhaps particularly in the Old Testament, that is exclusively archaic. The precise limits of the tribal boundaries (Josh. 14:1–19:51), the trial by ordeal (Num. 5:11-31), the regalia of the high priest (Exod. 39:1 ff.) and much else, are only of antiquarian interest to us. So the answer to question 7 can be: Nothing at all. If you give this answer you do not, of course, use the text as the basis of preaching and instruction in the church.

This word "church" in our question brings us to the vexed and perpetual question of the authority of the Old Testament for the Christian community. Is the Old Testament obsolete for the Christian to whom God has spoken in these last days by his Son? Or, at the other extreme, is the Old Testament always and everywhere about Jesus Christ, whose person, gospel, and church are concealed behind the outward events described and perceptible to the eye of faith? Or is the Old Testament the elementary-school part of the education of the children of God, who have now graduated from it, although they must sometimes be reminded of their first lessons? These are the three "classical" answers to the problem of the Old Testament in the church.[4]

We are here proceeding on the assumption (otherwise we would not have set out on the long road into Naboth's vineyard) that the church has been correct in seeing the Old Testament as somehow God's word to his people in all the ages. It was addressed first of all and specifically to Israel. But since he is God and not man, consistent in his person and activity, his word is not otherwise to us. He moves among his people; he leaves his footprints and the memories of these movements. As he speaks to and through Abraham, Moses, Elijah, Isaiah, Ahab, Sennacherib, Cyrus, he also speaks to and through us.

Therefore, what he says in I Kings 21 he says to us. There are inherent rights among God's children which the tyrant can neither abrogate nor overwhelm. There is in the possession and uses of power a perpetual temptation to run roughshod over these rights. When this temptation is not resisted the immediate goal of the aggressor may be secured, perhaps through murder and raw power, but he still has to face the God of history. This God never leaves himself without his witnesses. Elijah was such a witness. Naboth's vineyard is a plot of land which can be mapped, and this map also describes many other plots of land. As long as there is such a place of infamy, there is need for the word of the Lord by the hand of Elijah.

It is obvious that the preacher cannot attempt for every sermon the kind of historical and exegetical study I have undertaken here. Nor is it suggested that my historical and exegetical judgments are all entirely correct and incapable of challenge. What I have sought to set forth is a model for the kind of serious Bible study that should be presupposed when one makes a claim to be a minister of the word. Much of this material should be the common property of all who have been educated for the ministry and wear the degree master of divinity. But the kind of knowledge one carries from the platform where his degree has been awarded cannot be retained—let alone deepened, enlarged, and enriched—if serious Bible study ends with the parchment. Continuing education which focuses entirely on counseling, communicating, and administrative skills to the neglect of theology, history, and (at least in the Reformed tradition) above all the Bible, will not produce for the church a ministry that can help the people grow in understanding of divine revelation.

Effective preaching and teaching, however, require more than antiquarian and exegetical expertise. Something has to be added to knowledge. And that something is the preacher's vision of truth and reality which comes to him through his immersion in the present life of his own people as well as in Scripture. As a Bible teacher he needs to be a photographer, setting forth what is there. But he needs also to be an artist and portrait painter, adding to an accurate picture of what is there his own vision of truth and reality. It is not enough for him to translate and repeat what is on the print and paper that make up our Bibles. A good modern translation will do that. Why should I retell the story of Naboth and his vineyard? The narrator in I Kings 21 does it with simplicity, style, power—I cannot duplicate it, let alone improve on it. For me simply to retell the story, and burden it with my exegetical, linguistic, and archaeological learning and expertise, will only "darken counsel" even if the words be with knowledge.

What I see in I Kings 21 is how God looks upon the kind of scene that is there portrayed. What I hear is what God says in the face of the kind of violation of the second commandment that is described. Naboth's vineyard is the scene of a tragedy, but it is not a unique scene. Naboth's vineyard is often found, and in many places. The players, the scenery, and the words spoken will change, but the lines of the plot run in the same melancholy direction. Good biblical preaching will take the story from the streets of Jezreel to the streets of Lakeport. We cannot emphasize too strongly, however, how important it is to know as much as we can about what happened in Jezreel and how the people who gave us the Bible viewed the event. It is sound preliminary study which can make topical preaching truly biblical and save us from making the Bible merely a mirror for reflecting our own constellation of prejudices. At the same time we must be on guard against making it the means of exhibiting our own learning. The hazards of homiletical navigation are the reefs and rocks of antiquarian irrelevancy and the winds and tides of topical opinion and prejudice.

The sermon is not the only vehicle of biblical truth. From early times in Christian history, the

Bible has been presented in the form of drama. Most of us can remember the dressing-gowned wise men and bed-sheeted shepherds of Sunday school Christmas pageants and plays. It is easy and cheap to put this kind of thing down. Certainly the participants benefit from their work and fun together and their exposure to the words of the gospels. At the other end of the sophistication scale we get a full drama like Archibald Mac-Leish's *J.B.*, a play in which the story of Job and the dialogues of that book are put in terms of modern mid-America.[5]

In the next chapter we are going to see the story of I Kings 21 in a modern dramatic presentation. And in the chapter following, the events of the drama are going to be assumed to have happened. That chapter will be a sermon in which a modern prophet brings I Kings 21 to bear on that event.

5 I KINGS 21 - A ONE-ACT PLAY - GARY N. JOHNSTON

Description of the Characters

WILLIE MAE MCNEE, octogenarian widow of the
late Thomas McNee, has somewhat accidentally
become a member of the Hynes Heights University community. Some University trustees mis-
takenly believed that Thomas McNee had been
a wealthy man. In pecuniary hope they had
made his widow an honorary member of the
faculty club. In fact her husband, whose craft

had been the restoring and rebinding of old and rare books, had died leaving her little besides the house that she owns. She lives on her old-age security pension and the proceeds of a small annuity. Her house is located very close to the campus—in fact it is directly in line with the direction in which university expansion must next move. It is this fact that creates the drama we are about to witness.

Mrs. McNee treasures her faculty club privilege very much indeed. Every fine day she sits on a bench on the campus near the club. Every day she has her lunch in the club. Her presence is somewhat of a nuisance to the president of the university. In fact Dr. Marsden now goes to lunch when he sees Willie Mae leaving. Eccentric of bearing and dress, stiff with arthritis, friendly and talkative, Mrs. McNee has become a kind of campus fixture—indeed she is almost as much a landmark as

IRENE McFALL, the real ruler of the university. Now in her seventies, Miss McFall began her association with H.H.U. as a lecturer in English. She decided early in her academic career that administration, not teaching, was to be her vocation, so she took a leave of absence for a few years while she qualified herself in both educational theory and business administration. She returned to the campus as a special assistant to the president, with responsibility for the development of the physical plant. She attached herself to J. L. Brandywine, a construction tycoon who combined a sincere interest in education with his own business interests. How far Irene's attachment to J. L. extended beyond business association was a matter of perpetual speculation but no real knowledge. It was a discreet association. Irene and J. L. managed to have a series of weak, figurehead presidents appointed, and thus for decades they were the real rulers of the university. For the past fifteen years, however, there has been a somewhat more impressive president in the person of Edward Marsden. Early in the Marsden incumbency, Irene's influence went into temporary decline. But he is now approaching retirement, and Irene is asserting herself again. She has managed to revive Brandywine's interest by promising him that the next building, a theater-auditorium, will be named after him. Despite her age, Irene always look sharp, neat, impressive—she seems to be eternally emerging from beauty parlors!

J. L. BRANDYWINE, a stereotype tycoon in his early seventies. He is perhaps four years younger than Irene, under whose magnetic influence he has now been for four decades. He was married in his late thirties. His compulsive work habits and his attachment to Irene resulted in a divorce. He never remarried. In recent months the completion of the university expansion program has consumed his revived power of concentration and work. He believes that the theater-auditorium will be named after him.

EDWARD MARSDEN is sixty-five and about to retire. He has been president for fifteen years now. He wants to get the final phase of the expansion program out of the way as expeditiously as possible. He would dearly love to bring his incumbency to a peaceful and triumphant conclusion.

DAN SWEENEY is but thirty-seven, and thus half the average age of the others in this group. He has been chairman of the board of trustees for two years, and, to Irene's dismay, he has refused to be a passive, titular chairman. He has refused to identify progress solely with building expansion. Because of his competence and connections, Irene has been unable to dispense with him. Since money for education is becoming much tighter, the kind of skill that Sweeney has (he is an actuary) is imperative. His main purpose is to bring costs under control without sacrificing adequate faculty salaries and without raising fees beyond the reach of less advantaged students.

The Cast   Mrs. Willie Mae McNee
Miss Irene McFall
Mr. J. L. Brandywine
Mr. Edward Marsden
Mr. Dan Sweeney

The Setting   All the events of this play take place in two localities. The first scene is a bench somewhere on the campus of Hynes Heights University —probably very near the faculty club, where Mrs. McNee goes to eat lunch every noon. The other scene is the plush and comfortable office of the university president, Dr. Marsden. This office is very nicely laid out with executive-suite furniture. It is located high in the central campus structure—the administration building. In all directions from the this central structure the university has been systematically expanded according to the McFall-Brandywine plan. The president's window overlooks the southern expansion of the university and the future site of the one remaining unfinished part—a theater-auditorium to be named after J. L. Brandywine. But this fact is not visible to the audience and must be described elsewhere. In this office is an easel with diagrams, charts, financial figures, dates, and other data related to the final phase of expansion. Near the center of the office is a large board-room table. Upon this table is a clay model of the completed university. This model is propped up at an angle from the table so the audience can see it. One part of this model layout is colored bright red, while all else is white. The red area is the house of Mrs. Willie Mae McNee and the proposed site of the Brandywine theater-auditorium complex, the only uncompleted phase of the expansion. Also sitting on the table is a plastic model of the theater-auditorium in white.

SCENE I

This scene opens with Willie Mae's bench near the front center part of the stage. It is brightly lit. As the lights come up on the stage, Mrs. McNee is seen entering from the left area of the stage. She moves slowly but steadily in the direction of the bench. She appears to be unaware of an audience and very intent upon her walking. She is in all her glory with her white shoes, beret, a brooch of the national flag, and a walking stick. Just before reaching the bench she stops and goes into her resting pose; she places her hand on her hip and looks all about her with her eyeglasses down on her nose somewhat. Plenty of time should be allowed in these first few moments for the audience to take in every detail of Willie Mae's attire and characteristic movements. These are very important parts of her character. She gives no indication that she is aware of the audience, although she may look directly at them, making them feel that she could be looking at them individually. One of Mrs. McNee's habits is to squint her eyes and pucker her lips slightly while in this standing-resting posture. She is at once likable, comical, real, and lovable. After pausing a few moments in this standing position, Mrs. McNee laughs to herself and then speaks.

WILLIE MAE *(laughing and chuckling to herself, gesturing toward the bench)*: Now they've gone and moved that bench. *(Stands laughing, musing to herself somewhat below her breath, shaking her head.)* I told that young man to leave that bench alone; that's my bench and I need to have it right where I want it. *(Willie Mae begins to move toward the bench again, still musing to herself and chuckling.)* I'll just have to have lunch with that nice young man again, that Dr. Marsden. He'll see to it that they leave my bench alone. He's such a nice fellow. I remember when that chemistry professor was fired and they hired that nice young man, that Dr. Marsden—he's been such a lovely president. *(She speaks these words carefully and clearly, want-*

*ing to convince her invisible audience that Mars-
den is nice and lovely.)* Of course, it took them
a few years to find a nice fellow like him *(she
laughs)*—took them thirty years as a matter of
fact! *(She has reached the front of the bench
and now seems to be debating whether or not
to sit down. She eyes the bench, then eyes
everyone and everything around very carefully,
then begins the obviously difficult and painful
process of sitting down on the bench. This sitting
process requires her full attention and energy,
and it takes her a moment to get herself oriented
once she has actually completed the process.
Finally, and again very slowly, Willie Mae
crosses her legs with a bit of grimacing and
pain. This all done, she now looks directly at all
parts of the audience, very seriously, sometimes
over the top of her drooping glasses. Suddenly
she looks almost angry, wrinkles up her nose,
and frowns at the audience. This is followed by
the kind of face that a child would make. She
repeats the face once or twice. She looks very
silly doing this, but is undeterred by laughter
from the audience. Just as suddenly, she stops
making faces and looks away from the audience
very nonchalantly, as though she is unaware of
them having any significance for her. Then she
looks back at them angrily.)* Well, what do you
want? Humpf! *(Then she smiles very pleasantly
and begins talking cosily as if she were at tea*

94

with friends.) That reminds me. The other day I received a call from this lovely Dr. Marsden, and he wondered if I might not be free to come over and have a chat with him, and then maybe go and have lunch with him at the faculty club. Well, I told him that I thought that might be all right, provided he didn't get going on how much he needed my house. He's such a nice young man, but he does seem to carry on much more than I care for him to about what a nice man my husband was. *(Angrily)* Of course my husband—the late Mr. Thomas McNee—was a nice man! What does he think? That I'd marry a man who wasn't nice? *(chuckling and smiling.)* I should think not. Well that's neither here nor there. *(She laughs again. Now she begins to talk with a rather serious, business-like tone of voice.)* Things have changed so much around here the last fifty years that I can hardly believe my eyes. *(She points off to the right.)* See that building over there? They call that thing the Central Administration and Student Union Building. Humpf! *(she laughs)* Looks like a fat flagpole to me! *(She is pleased with her little joke.)* I remember when they used to have the most lovely little stand of trees and a garden where that . . . flagpole! . . . is now. *(She laughs again and shakes her head.)* Now Dr. Marsden tells me that they are going to have to expand the university even more and build more things

95

like that! *(She is obviously disdainful of the intrusion of modern buildings into an area she remembers as peaceful, wooded, unsophisticated.)* We'll see about that! *(She pauses for a bit, staring off for a little while. She looks over the top of her glasses at the audience again.)* I suppose that I had better be on my way if I'm to keep my appointment. I told you, didn't I, about my appointment with Dr. Marsden? Anyway, that's where I'm headed. *(She scoots up to the front of the bench placing her hands on both of her knees. She smiles and holds this pose for a few minutes.)* He's not fooling me though. I know that he only wants to offer me some more money for my house! *(She laughs.)* Silly boy, he is. After all, I'm just a poor little old lady, and that house is the last thing which I have. *(She looks serious and, for the first time, a bit sad.)* He's too young to know about that, though. *(Willie Mae now stands up—somewhat easier and less dramatically than she sat down.)* I'll just tell him "no" again, just like I did the last time. Some day he'll quit asking. *(The audience would expect her to laugh at this point, but she does not laugh, only looks very serious, then reaches around for her cane and purse and begins to walk off to the left of the stage. She stops for a moment, turns and looks back at the audience. Smiles, a big smile, as though she has a secret.)* If Thomas were here he would tell that Dr. Marsden and his boys to go jump in the lake. *(She laughs loudly, continues to laugh while looking at the audience; then she becomes serious again and smiles slightly.)* Oh, well *(she starts walking off stage again)* I'll be a little nicer to them than Thomas wouid have been. *(She disappears off stage and is heard shuffle along and mumbling to herself a little.)*

The lights come up on Dr. Marsden's office in another area of the stage. Marsden and Brandywine are laughing very hard at each other, slapping each other on the back, and generally carrying on. They appear to have drinks in their hands.

MARSDEN: The Thomas McNee Center for the Lively Arts! *(Laughs and continues laughing)* I've got to hand it to Irene. What a wit! *(Laughing.)*

BRANDYWINE *(laughing too)*: Why can't we think of things like that, Ed? It takes a woman with her kind of ingenuity to think of a thing like that! *(Laughing and carrying on)*.

MARSDEN *(still laughing, but not so hard)*: What do you suppose she has up her sleeve today, J. L.?

BRANDYWINE *(laughter coming to an end)*: Whatever it is, you can bet it's original. I've never known Irene to be beaten by anyone *(looking very serious)*—not anyone! *(He takes a drink, the last swallow in his glass. Puts his glass down on the desk and moves over to the layout, studying it.)* Just think, Ed, we've almost done it. This is quite a monument! Don't you agree, Ed?

MARSDEN: Sure do, J. L. But it's not done yet, you know. It all depends on Mrs. McNee now *(he walks over to Brandywine and puts his hand on his shoulder)* . . . and Irene. *(He walks back toward the desk.)* But Irene has pulled us out of jams like this before, and I'm damned sure she'll do it again this time. *(He takes a cigar and trims the end of it.)*

BRANDYWINE *(staring at the layout)*: The J. L. Brandywine Center for the Lively Arts! I never thought I'd live to see the day, Ed. It's quite an honor to have a thing like that named after you. I'm very honored. Very honored indeed. *(At this point the buzzer on the desk sounds. Marsden picks up the phone to receive a message from his secretary. He places the phone down.)*

MARSDEN: Mrs. McNee is here early, J. L. She wasn't supposed to be here for another thirty minutes. What shall we do? Irene is tied up in a meeting with Dan Sweeney and the board of trustees until two o'clock.

BRANDYWINE: Don't panic, Ed; that won't help at all. Go out there and ask her if she's had

98

lunch yet. If she hasn't, take her over to the club and give her lunch. By then Irene and Dan will be here. *(Marsden collects himself and disappears through a door to the outer office. He leaves the door slightly ajar so that the sound of voices can be heard. As soon as he leaves the office, Brandywine goes over to the telephone and begins to dial a number.)*

BRANDYWINE *(on the phone):* Hello? . . . hello . . . *(Marsden comes back into the office.)* Hold the line a minute, please. *(He cups his hand over the phone and addresses Marsden.)* Well, has she eaten yet?

MARSDEN: No, thank God. I'll take her to the club. See if you can get Irene and Dan out of that meeting so that they are waiting for us when we get back. *(Marsden starts to leave, then turns back.)* What shall I talk to her about, J. L.?

BRANDYWINE: Talk to her about the Thomas McNee Center for the Lively arts! *(They both laugh at this, and Marsden leaves the room.)*

BRANDYWINE *(back on the phone):* Are you still on the line? Good. *(He now sits in Marsden's executive chair. He looks very comfortable and "tycoonish" in this position.)* Now tell me what's going on there this morning. *(He listens very closely, scribbles a note on a pad on the desk.)* No soap, huh? What's the highest offer you made? *(Shows shock at the figure he hears.)*

They're a bunch of damn fools . . . Well, what do you recommend now? (*He listens closely and with a look of astonishment and disbelief on his face.*) But I really don't know if it's worth that. (*Pause.*) Do you know what would happen if anyone found out about this? (*Pause.*) Are you sure of legalities? (*Pause.*) O.K. Just sit tight until you hear from me again. There's one last chance that Dr. McFall will come up with something this afternoon, and I'm sure as hell hoping that she does. (*Pause.*) I don't know, but don't you make a move until you hear from me. Do you understand? (*He hangs up the phone, then gets up and walks around until he is in front of the plaster model, takes the model of the theater-auditorium off the table and places it on the layout. He stares at it a few moments. Then he shakes his head.*) It just isn't worth it. It just isn't worth it. (*He grabs the model of the theater-auditorium from the layout and throws it into a nearby wastebasket.*) There goes the J. L. Brandywine Center for the Lively Arts, thanks to a little old lady. Why in God's name did her husband have to build that house right there? (*The door to the office opens, and in comes Dr. Irene McFall. She shuts the door behind her and begins to move, slowly but with agility, using her cane, toward the front of the desk. While moving she speaks.*)

McFALL: Hello, J. L. (*She looks at him with just*

a glance, but her glance takes in all there is to see. Irene misses very little.)

BRANDYWINE: You're here early, Dr. McFall. Is the trustee meeting over already?

MCFALL: Oh, heaven's sake, no. It'll go on for another hour at least. Where's Dr. Marsden? He's supposed to be here for this little meeting too.

BRANDYWINE: Mrs. McNee got here early, so he took her to the faculty club for lunch to kill time until you and Dan could get here.

MCFALL *(She has finally reached the front of the desk where she stops and looks all around to determine where everything is, and to get some idea of what may have been happening. She even glances into the wastebasket and sees the model of the theater-auditorium there. J. L. does not catch this. But he does notice that she is bending over, very slowly, to get something. Then it is obvious that she is retrieving the model from the wastebasket. She does so, handles it, studies it.)* I assume that this just fell in there! Really, J. L., we've been *(she pauses and hesitates)* . . . friends . . . *(looks directly at him)* long enough that I know when things are not going well. Now let's just sit down here and go over a few things. *(She motions toward two chairs in front of the desk, and with care and geriatric style she moves into one of them herself. J. L. does not move; he stands still, looking almost like a boy who has just been scolded.)*

BRANDYWINE: It isn't going to work, Irene. I can feel it. That old lady just isn't going to give in, and none of our tricks have worked yet.

MCFALL *(motioning to the other chair):* Sit down, please! *(He does so, rather awkwardly.)* Now, what's all this nonsense about? *(Irene often has to push her glasses back, and while she does so, she grimaces. She is a tall woman with precise posture and always holds her head as it should be held, chin tilted slightly upward.)*

BRANDYWINE: Irene, I've been in the construction business for over forty years now, and I've literally built this university from just one little building to the seventy-eight structures we now have. *(He gets up, moves over to a drawer in Marsden's desk where liquor is kept.)* But I have never *(leaning with both fists on the desk toward Irene)* done anything illegal.

MCFALL: Well, now, aren't you the righteous one? And what, may I ask, has brought about this sudden purity of conviction and motivation? *(She changes her voice some.)* I must say, I haven't noticed it before now.

BRANDYWINE *(He has fished a bottle out of the drawer and pours himself a drink; he takes a swallow. Irene is looking cool, collected—she studies him very quietly and passively while he takes his drink and thinks about what she has*

102

been saying.): Irene, you know how badly I want to see this project completed, once and for all. We have been talking for thirty years about building the theater-auditorium as the climax of all our planning and construction. The first building was to be called "The McFall Center for Classical Studies." *(J. L. has been moving about the room, obviously acting out some past dreams and conversations, with only a hint of present events having intervened.)* And there it sits *(he points to a building on the layout)*— completed in 1942, the very first unit in the expansion plan, named after *(he gestures eloquently toward her)* Dr. Irene McFall. And now, the final building *(he picks up the model of the theater-auditorium from the desk)*—the J. L. Brandywine Center for the Lively Arts. I understand that the bronze name plaque, twenty feet long, four feet high, has already been ordered. *(He sets the model back down.)* And now, after thirty years, I am told that there will be no building because a little old lady named Willie Mae McNee is too in love with the house that her husband built her to give it up for money, bribery, threat, or J. L. Brandywine. You know, Irene, this thing has driven me mad, I do believe. You won't believe what I've had my lawyer doing this morning.

McFALL: Just a minute now, J. L. I think you should remember that things aren't over yet.

103

You talk like we have all decided just to lay down and let this little old McNee woman run over us like a steamroller. Well, that just isn't so, and you ought to know by now, J. L., that this is not the way it is going to be. And as for this business with your lawyers this morning, I can rather imagine what you have been up to behind the scenes, J. L. *(She gets up and moves in the direction of a table with a small coffeepot on it near the desk. She stops and looks directly at him after getting up and pushes her glasses up, as she has done all along, only this time it emphasizes what she is going to say.)* I may be old, J. L., but I'm not getting stupid. All this stuff about you not doing anything . . . "illegal." . . . I think it was illegal, was it not? The word you used, "illegal." . . Well, anyway—all this talk about how innocent and aboveboard you have been in your dealings over these many years. Well, it all depends on what you want to define as legal. My guess is that you had your lawyers downtown trying to bribe the city commissioners into condemning poor old Willie Mae's house and property, and then donating it to the city for your new building. *(She laughs, and begins to walk toward the coffeepot again, laughing and talking as she moves.)* Oh, J. L., you and your little, shall we say, "legalities"! *(She arrives at the coffeepot and turns to look at him again.)* Well, I did guess it, J. L.? *(But he just turns his back and walks away, taking another swallow from his glass.)* Now listen here, J. L. We've tried that route before, and it doesn't work. *(She has poured a cup of coffee and is looking around for cream and sugar.)* Where does Ed keep his cream and sugar? Do you know, J. L.? *(She is now devoting her attention to finding these ingredients, shuffling around the desk. J. L. reluctantly moves over to help her, goes to a drawer, and takes out a jar of powdered cream and a jar of sugar without comment; he then sits in the executive chair behind the desk while Irene finishes doctoring her coffee)* Thank you, I just need a spoonful of each. Do you care for coffee, J. L.?

BRANDYWINE: No, thank you.

McFALL *(takes her coffee and begins to move back in the direction of the chair in which she had been sitting earlier):* Now, what was I saying? Oh, yes, we've been to city hall before, J. L., and they know very well what problems we are having in getting that McNee property to finish our expansion. We can't depend on them to help us one little bit, you know that. *(She sits down and takes a sip.)* So I've been looking at this a little differently and had my people working on another angle. . . . This coffee is terrible, must have been brewed yesterday. *(She takes another sip, then moves over toward the*

105

pot apparently to dispose of the coffee. Instead she adds more cream and sugar.)

BRANDYWINE: Just what angle have you been pursuing, Irene?

McFALL *(She smiles a bit, looks at him, chuckles.):* I don't know if I should tell you or not, Mr. Brandywine. *(Laughing.)* After all, you don't know anything about . . . illegalities. *(A silent pause as it appears that McFall is going to keep her plans to herself or at least find out just how curious J. L. really is. She moves again to her chair, sits down, and drinks her coffee.)* By the way, just how much money did you offer the commissioners this morning, J. L.?

BRANDYWINE *(in a low voice, obviously embarrassed about the amount):* fifty thousand dollars each and a 20 percent kickback on any future building contracts that my company gets from the city.

McFALL: Oh, J. L., that's too much. You're such a silly man sometimes. *(Pause.)* Well, what did you propose to do after that deal fell through this morning?

BRANDYWINE *(surprised by this question):* How did you know that I had another plan?

McFALL: I didn't. I was just guessing. But now that you've confirmed my guess, would you like to tell me about it? After all, we started this thing together, J. L.; we might as well finish

106

together. Don't you agree? *(She looks very serious.)*

BRANDYWINE: Actually, Irene, it wasn't my idea at all, and I haven't decided what to do about it anyway. I'd just as soon forget about it because I don't think it's such a good idea now.

McFALL *(laughing derisively)*: Oh boy, you must have a real pleasant scheme on your hands this time, J. L. *(Drinks her coffee.)* Well, let's have it, no use keeping it to yourself. *(Pause. She studies him closely as he appears unwilling to share his plan.)* Is it murder, J. L.?

BRANDYWINE *(turns around and looks at her, hands in pockets, steps toward her and laughs a bit foolishly)*: Oh, Irene, all these years and you don't know me any better than that? *(He begins walking toward her, his age apparent in his unsteady gait.)* I wish that I could believe that you are kidding me, Irene, but I've known you forty years too long to believe it. You actually do believe that I would murder a helpless old lady just so I could have a building named after me? *(He sits on the edge of the table, slightly just behind but near McFall; he folds his hands across his chest and shakes his head, looks very saddened; his voice is lower and weaker now.)* You know what really makes me sad, Irene? *(Looks directly at her, leans over, placing his hand on her chair.)*

McFALL *(not looking at him)*: I suppose you'll

107

tell me, whether I want to hear it or not, J. L., so go ahead.

BRANDYWINE: Tell me something honestly, Irene. What is more important to you—that this new theater-auditorium be named after me? Or that the expansion program which you started all those years ago be finished? After all, I'm sure that you are aware that people are already talking about naming the whole university after you when you retire or die—(sarcastically) whichever comes first. What about it, Irene, whose interests are you looking out for—mine or your own?

McFALL: That's a foolish question, J. L., and I am greatly hurt that you would even suggest such a thing. In all my years of association with this university—even when I was a lowly English instructor—my interest has always been what is best for the students and community which we serve. You ought to know that better than anyone else, J. L. And as for naming these buildings and university, that is none of my affair. You know how those decisions are made. It was decided long ago that your indispensable contributions to the growth and development of this university were deemed sufficient to merit your name being placed on the most advanced and well-equipped and glamorous building of all. And, as for the university being named after me *(she looks directly at him now, seriously, angrily)* I couldn't care less, and I would be engaging in the silliest and most useless folly to suggest that I could have any say in such a suggestion. *(Getting up from her chair.)* You're such a silly man sometimes, J. L. *(She begins to move back toward the coffeepot.)* I'm beginning to think that we should name the new theater-auditorium the Thomas McNee Center for the Lively Arts!

BRANDYWINE *(now standing near the center of the office, glasses in hand, reflecting very seriously on what has taken place):* So now what, Irene? What do we do now in the best interest of the students and the community? *(Sits down, burying his head a little in his hands. He looks very saddened and put down.)*

McFALL *(She has poured another cup of coffee and is doctoring it.):* I should think the "what now," as you put it, is very obvious. As the most influential of the trustees, you know that the university and the community want the auditorium, and want it to be built where Mrs. Willie Mae McNee has her house. So, we must see that the wishes of the university and the community are implemented. *(Shuffles back to her chair, takes a sip of coffee; she is now fully in charge again.)* In other words, J. L., you, J. L. Brandywine, want the property on which this house sits, for the university. *(Takes an-*

other sip.) And now, if you will just leave this whole matter to me, I'll see that you get it.

SCENE II

Mrs. McNee and Dr. Marsden are seated
on the bench.

McNEE: That was so thoughtful of you, Dr. Marsden, to invite me to lunch. It was a lovely lunch, and I want to thank you very much.

MARSDEN: Not at all, Mrs. McNee. It was the very least that I could do for you. You have been very gracious over these many years, and your presence on our campus is a source of delight to all the students with whom you have chatted.

McNEE: Well, I do enjoy talking with the young boys and girls who come here. They are such lovely young people—but not like the young people who used to come here before you started making this big school. *(She pats Marsden on the hand, and begins to talk to him in a grand-motherly way.)* I hope that you don't mind a bit of advice from an old lady, but I must say that I think the school has gotten much too big to be the sociable little place that it once was. *(Now reminiscing.)* It used to be that I could sit here on this bench and within two hours say a "hello" to every student here. My, that was a lovely time then. *(She begins to get a little carried away, lecturing Marsden, gesturing with her cane.)* But now you've gone and built all these funny-looking . . . edifices *(smiles and chuckles a bit),* and no one sees anyone. *(Gesturing with her cane.)* See how they run around here without seeing each other, just like a bunch of racing cars. I haven't had the opportunity to speak with a young person here on this bench in over a year. They all just pass me by and don't even see me. *(Chuckling again, very amused.)* You know, Dr. Marsden, I even tried to trip one of them with my cane two months ago, just so that he would stop and say something to me, but he just stepped over it and never even said so much as "how do you do." *(Pause.)* Of course, I'm just an old lady now, and they aren't interested in old ladies.

MARSDEN: I wish I had your luck, Mrs. McNee. These students don't leave me alone at any time. And I agree—they have changed. They used to respect the president of the university—whatever he said decided matters. Not now. Now they want to be trustees of the university, to be on the academic counsel, to hire and fire professors. They want to decide which dormitories should be built where, and who should live in them. I have at least two student groups a week come and see me in my office with a petition about one thing or another. Last week it was about the food in the cafeterias, next week it will probably be about parking lots. Maybe you should come and sit outside of my office and talk with the students. It would take a lot of pressure away from me.

McNEE: No, Dr. Marsden, they don't want to talk with me. These young people are right, you know. They should be heard. The problem is that you've made such a huge place that no one gets heard unless they shout or make a big fuss. My husband, Thomas McNee, and I used to have students come and have dinner with us in the evening at least twice a week. In a year's time we had every student in our house for dinner at least once. Thomas used to love that, Dr. Marsden—sometimes he would stay up until two or three in the morning talking with students. *(She has slipped back into her own world, no longer aware of his presence.)* Thomas was such a good man. He used to say to me, "Now, Willie Mae, don't you tease these young people. They need to be taken seriously." So I had my instructions not to make fun of them, but to listen to them. Thomas was not an educated man, but he used to read books and books and books just so that he could talk intelligently with the students. And they respected his opinions. Of course, Thomas was a very brilliant man in his own field. He was the foremost expert and

authority in the world on the restoration and
care of old and rare books. He even received
a citation from L'Université de Paris *(she says
this proudly, correctly pronouncing the French
words)* for his outstanding work on the rare
books collection there.

MARSDEN: Yes, I recall your having told me that
once before, Mrs. McNee. How long is it now
since your husband died?

MCNEE *(looking directly at him, very seriously)*:
Nine years, three months, and four days. He
would have been seventy-four next month.

MARSDEN: You miss him very much . . .

MCNEE *(now back to her humorous self)*: Do I
miss Thomas? Well now, that's a fine question
for a young fellow like you to be asking. Why,
Thomas is much better off than I am now, Dr.
Marsden. He just up and died and got himself
out of all this mess. *(Gestures with a cane at
the surrounding buildings.)* And now I have to
stay here by myself and look at what a mess
all this is becoming. *(Very dramatic, making
faces, grimacing and with much disdain and
scorn in her voice—she is actually having a lot
of fun talking this way.)* Of course, I wouldn't
want you to be offended. After all, it wasn't your
idea to build this place the way it is. We both
know *(She says this quietly, confidentially)* that
it was that Dr. McFall *(now very loudly, with
a big gesture)*—Irene McFall. *(She laughs.)*

113

That's what this place will be called when she finally dies. The Irene McFall University. (*She stops this very abruptly, gets serious again.*) Well, that's neither here nor there. Poor old Thomas does not have to sit here on this bench and see all of this. (*Laughs, looking at Marsden.*) Of course, I don't always have such a nice young man to sit with here and listen to this old lady carry on. (*Pats him on the hand again.*) You've been doing the best you can, young man. Just don't let that old . . . witch! (*much expression, nose wrinkled*) . . . shove you around. You've got lots of good ideas up there in that head (*touching him playfully on the head*). I just hope it isn't too late. (*Pause, looking around.*) I mean, it would be a shame to tear some of these buildings down. They cost too much, and people would say that it was a terrible waste.

MARSDEN (*feeling patronized*): I can assure you, Mrs. McNee, there are no plans to tear down any of the buildings—except maybe the old gymnasium so that we can build a better one— but that's a long way off yet. (*Pause, proceeding cautiously.*) In fact . . . we have been hoping to add another new building—one which the university needs very much.

McNEE (*She is totally uninterested in this—she is still daydreaming back in her own world, and suddenly becomes aware that Marsden has stopped talking.*): Well, I'll tell you this, Dr.

114

Marsden—you won't be building anything new where my house is. *(Looks at him over the top of her glasses.)* So if you are thinking of offering me more money for my house, you can just forget it.

MARSDEN *(His face falls; he realizes he shouldn't have raised the issue just now.):* Yes, I recall that the last time we talked—about a month ago—you told me the same thing. But some things have taken place in the meantime which I think you may be interested in learning about.

McNEE: I doubt that very much. *(She says this very softly, nonchalantly—not appearing to notice the anxiety that has been stirred up in Marsden. Suddenly she turns and looks at him very angrily.)* All you people here ever think about anymore is tearing down and building more. *(Now quietly again)* You ought to think about using what you already have. When was the last time you ever sat down to talk with a student? I'll bet you don't even know the names of ten students.

MARSDEN *(now becoming more assertive, somewhat pompous):* Mrs. McNee, I know the names of many of my students, and my wife and I frequently have them in our home for dinner. I appreciate your concern for the future of the university and the problems that accompany growth and progress. All of us would do well to spend more time listening to each other. But

115

there is also a responsibility to plan for the future and to be prudent and wise in making a place for young people of the future to study and to equip themselves for living in a rapidly changing world. I am sure that you appreciate that fact—as your husband would if he were still alive. Here at Hynes Heights University we have been fortunate in having a well-planned and systematic program of expansion and growth. And it is to Dr. McFall's credit that she and Mr. Brandywine, nearly thirty years ago, were able to dream what you see about you now. You are right, Mrs. McNee, it is a different place than it was when your husband and you used to entertain students in your home. *(A long pause during which Dr. Marsden has risen from the bench and is walking behind it, up and down, pensively.)* I hope that you will give that some thought, Mrs. McNee.

McNee *(very lightly):* You needn't give me a pep talk, Dr. Marsden. *(Pause.)* Besides, I may not want to think about it. *(She says this defiantly).* You young fellows should think about that! *(Smiles to herself. Marsden cannot see this smile as he is still behind her.)*

Marsden *(more to himself than to Willie Mae):* It's strange that J. L. Brandywine and Irene McFall are in the same generation as you, and yet you have nothing in common except your ages.

116

(He has returned to the front of the bench and has sat down.)

McNEE *(looks directly at him, smiles indulgently, pats his hand):* Now you mustn't take all this so seriously. Some day soon I'll die and then you can have my house and that will be all there is to that. *(Laughs.)* After all, Dr. Marsden, I won't live forever.

MARSDEN: You're right, Mrs. McNee, I still do want your house. And so do Dr. McFall and Mr. Brandywine and the trustees of the university. But we don't want you to have to die for us to get it. *(Pause.)* We've talked about all this before, though, so there is no point in discussing it again right here.

McNEE: There is no point in discussing it again anywhere, Dr. Marsden. Thomas built that house himself before there even was a university here, and he told me before he died that I should keep it and not sell it to anyone. He said, "Willie Mae, this house is paid for and it's full of all the the good memories and times which we have had together. Don't let anyone take it from you, Willie Mae, it's all the inheritance I have for you." Those are his exact words. And I intend to keep my inheritance, Dr. Marsden, and not you, nor J. L. Brandywine, nor Irene McFall, nor the board of trustees, will get that house from me. *(In a loud voice)* And that is that! *(Stamps her cane on the ground.)*

117

SCENE III

Back in Marsden's office.

McFALL: Come in, Dan, come in. *(Dan Sweeney has just entered the room.)*

BRANDYWINE: Mr. Sweeney, just in time. Dr. Marsden and Mrs. McNee should be here any minute now. How was the board meeting, Dan?

SWEENEY: They're all the same, Mr. Brandywine —long and tedious. We just finished reviewing the trust fund figures for next year, and it looks like we will have enough to begin with student grants a year sooner than expected.

BRANDYWINE: And just what does that mean, Dan?

SWEENEY: It means that there will be about one hundred fifty students next fall who will be attending university here who could not have afforded it otherwise. We will be subsidizing the full cost of university education for students who can demonstrate need—including spending money, housing, tuition, books, and food. All we ask is that they maintain a "C" average or better and repay half of the money at a time later in their lives when they can afford it— no interest charge. We have already received one hundred applications from high school seniors in Hynes Heights alone. The problem is going to be selection—there are far more

118

students who need and deserve these grants than we can presently provide for.

McFALL: Of course, you know what kind of student you are going to get with a program like that, don't you Mr. Sweeney?

SWEENEY: Dr. McFall, you have made it very clear in board meetings that you are opposed to such a program because it could bring poorly motivated and delinquent young people into the university. Your objections have been given a fair hearing and have caused us to investigate the students who have filed applications with us —we have investigated them very, very thoroughly. You left the board meeting today before I provided the information which indicates that there are no data to support your presuppositions. The problem for these students is indeed economic and has nothing to do with social maladjustments—crime or violence. These are not delinquents. All our applicants have high test scores, excellent grades, and seemed well motivated in screening interviews.

McFALL: We'll see, Mr. Sweeney. I've been in this business a good deal longer than you, and I know that you cannot take a young person from a lower socioeconomic class, give him a living for four years, and not have troubles. But I'm willing to test your hypothesis. *(Moves to one of the easels with charts on it.)* Anyhow, this has nothing to do with our meeting here

119

today. *(Changes some of the charts around a bit.)* Mr. Sweeney, I think you should pay particular attention to these figures you see here. As an accountant you will appreciate the problem that we confront. As you can see we have two and a half million dollars in a trust fund over here *(motions to a figure on a chart),* but there are strings on that money, gentlemen. It has to be used in one year or it reverts to the government general fund for higher education. In other words, we won't get one tenth of that money unless we use it immediately.

BRANDYWINE: Haven't you seen these statistics, Mr. Sweeney?

SWEENEY: No, this is all new to me. This special trust fund has been under the management of the building and expansion committee, headed by Dr. McFall. Dr. Marsden has suggested that this fund could perhaps be transferred to the general expenditures of the university—discretionary funds of the board of trustees. That's why I'm here today.

McFALL: Well, that would be a very neat little trick. But that is not what that money is intended for. It is intended to be spent in building the new theater-auditorium. *(Shifts charts around so that there is now a graphic representation of the money in the trust fund being spent on the theater-auditorium.)* If we transferred it to the general expenditures, the money

120

would be spent on something else, and we would not have our theater-auditorium.

SWEENEY: But it is my understanding that the theater-auditorium cannot be built within a year because the land we are trying to acquire for the site is not yet available. Has that changed?

BRANDYWINE: Not yet, Dan, not yet.

McFALL: Mr. Sweeney, in a few minutes you will be meeting Mrs. Willie Mae McNee. She is the sole owner of the property which we need. We have offered her sums of money three times in excess of the market value of the property. We have even offered to have her house—which she values so much—moved to a new site which we would provide. All our efforts to acquire this land have so far come to nothing. We are still hoping that today Mrs. McNee may be persuaded to sell us this land. Time has run out. Either we start the new theater-auditorium within a month, or it will not be completed within a year's time.

SWEENEY: And just how are you planning to persuade Mrs. McNee?

McFALL: That's a good question, Mr. Sweeney. I think Dr. Marsden hoped that you could be of assistance and talk with the little lady. You have a reputation for being very gentle and persuasive with people. We have even gone so far as to draw up a proposal to name the new theater-auditorium after her late husband—

121

Thomas McNee. Her reluctance to part with her house seems to be tied up with a deathbed pledge that she would not sell it.

BRANDYWINE: We need that property, Dan. This is the last phase of our expansion program, and those of us who are now senior citizens want to see it finished in our lifetime. *(The door opens, and Mrs. McNee comes in with Dr. Marsden. There is silence—it appears that everyone is looking to Irene McFall to take the lead and get on with the business.)*

McFALL *(Directs Willie Mae to one of the chairs in front of the desk, sits down herself in the other. The other persons group around variously. Sweeney stands off by himself, quietly, looking at the charts, and then out of the window.)*: Mrs. McNee, I'll come right to the point. We're here today to talk about the property on which your home is sitting. We've talked about this before and have not been able to come to an agreement, so there is no point in beating around the bush . . .

McNEE *(starts to interrupt McFall)*: You just want to get rid of me so you can . . .

McFALL: Now wait just a minute and hear what I have to say before you reply. We all understand and appreciate why you are so reluctant to part with your home. Your husband was a fine man, and we cared a great deal for him. In fact, I have had his background and work investigated very thoroughly. Here is what we would like you to consider, Mrs. McNee— now hear me out. We will pay you double the market value of your home and property, and we will move your house to a new site not far from here. We will build the new theater-auditorium where your house now is, and we will name it "The Thomas McNee Center for the Lively Arts." *(Brandywine turns his back at this point.)* But that isn't all. We will also establish a new department to be housed in the same building—"The McNee Department of Bibliopegy"—that means the care and restoration of old and rare books. *(Pause.)* Well, now, haven't we made you a fine offer, Mrs. McNee?

McNEE: You are a sly one, Dr. McFall. You never run out of tricks, do you?

McFALL: I don't know what you are talking about, Mrs. McNee.

McNEE: You know perfectly well what I am talking about. You wouldn't really name a building after Thomas, and if you did you would change the name of it after I am gone. It's just a trick to get me to sell you my property. *(Laughs.)* Well, I'm not going to be tricked by you, Dr. McFall, or anyone else. My house is not for sale! And that is that. *(Silence follows this declaration. Willie Mae is sitting very calmly, half smiling, and looking directly at Brandywine which makes him so uneasy that*

123

he moves nervously behind the desk and sits down.)

McFALL *(visibly angry, but trying very hard, and succeeding, at remaining outwardly tactful and composed)*: Now look here, Mrs. McNee. You are leaving us with very few options. *(Stops, realizing this is being too assertive and may frighten Willie Mae into hardening her position still more.)* We have offered you far more money than your property is worth, promised to move your house—lock, stock, and barrel—to a new lot we will buy for you, as well as honor your husband as no one has been honored in the history of Hynes Heights University. I just cannot understand your unwillingness to cooperate with us. *(But Willie Mae is not flinching—she is as much in control as Queen Victoria at court.)* Would you mind telling us, Mrs. McNee, just what it is that you expect from us?

McNEE: All I want from you is to be left alone. *(McFall, now out of her chair, is walking in the direction of Sweeney.)*

McFALL: Would you mind talking with Mrs. McNee, Mr. Sweeney? She doesn't want to listen to the rest of us. *(Her look, directly at Sweeney, challenges him to get the university out of this impasse.)*

SWEENEY *(Moves very slowly toward Willie Mae's chair. She is watching him closely, but not looking daggers at him, as she does at Mc-Fall. He sits on the arm of the chair, takes Mrs. McNee's hand, and after a long pause, speaks.):* Mrs. McNee, I don't think we've met. My name is Dan Sweeney.

McNEE: Well, what's your offer, Mr. Sweeney? *(asking as if she really wants to know).*

SWEENEY: Mrs. McNee, I haven't been in on these discussions all along, and I don't know what it is about your home that you value so much. I'd like to know.

McNEE *(studies him in a silence, to determine if his interest is sincere, or another ploy, then speaks very proudly):* My house, Mr. Sweeney, was built by my husband, the late Thomas Mc-Nee, before there was even an idea of building a university here. Everything about it and around it reminds me of him and of many other memories, both good and bad. It is all the inheritance that this old lady has, Mr. Sweeney. I wouldn't expect the people here *(looking around at the others with loathing)* to understand the importance of it. *(Pause.)* But you could at least respect it. *(She says this as if it is her last word, quietly but firmly, then leans back into her chair as if all energy has left her. Sweeney gets up from the arm of her chair and returns to the window. Everyone except McNee is watching him, expecting him to say some decisive word to her, but he says nothing.)*

McFALL *(after a long silence and pause, watching Sweeney for some signal which doesn't come, moves in her direction, staring at him for a moment, then shrugs):* Well, what shall we do now? *(Sweeney still silent, she shuffles over toward Brandywine, looking at him as though he were a waste of space.)* Any ideas, J. L.? *(He shakes his head, so she shuffles over to Marsden.)* And what about you, Dr. Marsden, any suggestions? *(He shakes his head no, so she shuffles over to where Mrs. McNee is, but her back is to Willie Mae.)* So it would appear, Mrs. McNee, that you have won this time. *(Turns slowly, looks at her, chin in air.)* But I warn you that the niceties are over. *(Pause. Her glasses have slid down on her nose, and she looks over them.)* We shall have to acquire your property by other means. *(Silence, as a staring contest between McFall and McNee goes on. At last, Sweeney moves from the window over to Mrs. McNee; he extends his hand to her, speaking to her.)*

SWEENEY: Mrs. McNee, I'm sorry we brought you here today. May I take you home? *(She studies him for sincerity, then begins to get out of her chair, saying nothing. Sweeney escorts Willie Mae from the room on his arm. The others remain frozen, watching them. It is something like a death march, only McNee is leaving with*

*much pride, and with dignity and integrity in-
tact. The lights fade.)*

SCENE IV

It is the bench again, only it has been moved to
the down left area of the stage from its previous
center stage area. The light that illuminates it has
a definite bluish hue to it. McNee is sitting on the
bench. She is in all her glory with her patriotic
brooch, white beret, cane, white stockings, glasses
on her nose, white sweater. She is whistling some
unmelodious tune very lightly—or it could be an
imitation of bird calls. She seems totally unaware
of the audience; even if she were aware of them,
she would be completely unconcerned about their
presence. She stops her whistling after awhile and
looks at the audience, all parts of it, very casually,
with a warm smile on her face, eyes crinkled up a
bit. It is the same old Willie Mae, it seems. She
sounds, appears, and seems to be, in a good mood.

McNEE: Well *(looks at the audience again,
smiling)*, I suppose you are all wondering what
they did with me and my house. *(Looks serious,
as though she will give an explanation; then she
notices the bench on which she is sitting.)*
They've moved my bench again. *(Shakes her
head, smiles.)* I wish they would leave my bench

127

alone. *(Laughs a bit.)* Someone is always moving it now. *(She now reaches into her purse, takes out some scraps of paper, unfolds one. It is a newspaper clipping; rather worn and tattered and a bit yellowed. She handles it gently and looks it over, appears to be reading a portion of it.)* This is what they did to me. *(Holds clipping up, but not so anyone could really read it.)* It says that my husband, Thomas *(begins to look very sad and to refold the clipping)* . . . it says that my husband, Thomas, was a . . . bigamist. *(Looks very serious now.)* But I know better. Thomas was not a bigamist at all. *(Pauses as she puts the clipping back into her purse, then looks directly at the audience, looking as though this were the ultimate now, then she laughs.)* But I'm incompetent. *(Smiles knowingly.)* Dr. McFall told the newspaper to print this story about my husband. She is a very clever woman, you know. And when the newspaper would not retract the story I decided that I would have to go to every home and explain personally that it wasn't true. *(Looks serious still, and proud— quite proud.)* I started on the south side of the city and went door to door and explained to people that this story about my late husband was not true. *(Looks away, passively.)* Then one day a man came to the door and told me to get away, he didn't want to hear anything about all of this. *(Pause.)* Well, I left, but he called the police and they brought me here. *(Gets up from her bench slowly, and begins to shuffle very slowly off to the other side of the stage. She stops center stage, turns and looks directly at the audience.)* They said I was incompetent. *(Wrinkles up her nose and speaks loudly and angrily.)* But I know that word means "crazy"! Mr. Sweeney arranged for me to come and live here in this hospital. Mr. Sweeney helped me to sell my house too. *(Smiles.)* He's such a nice lad, Mr. Sweeney. He comes and gets me every weekend and takes me to visit the nice young couple who bought my house. Sometimes I stay overnight with them. *(A pause, a chuckle, a smile.)* My house hasn't changed a bit, and neither has Dr. McFall—she still wants the university to have it. But Mr. Sweeney has seen to it that they will never have it—he's such a clever man. *(Lights out.)*

6 NABOTH'S VINEYARD IS NOW LOCATED IN HYNES HEIGHTS: A SERMON

Mrs. Thomas McNee lived in the "rest home" for a little less than a year. Dan Sweeney had arranged for her admission in September. She died the following July. By a strange coincidence, J. L. Brandywine had predeceased her by a few days. His third coronary carried him swiftly away. The cause of Willie Mae's death was never quite clear. She just seems to have faded from the twilight and shadows into the darkness. Mrs. McNee was a founding member of Hynes Heights Denominational Church. But it happened that she was buried, not by Jeremy Brown her current pastor, but by Fred Farley, who had been the first minister of Hynes Heights and an old friend of Willie Mae.

After the Second World War, Farley had entered a seminary which provided an accelerated program for veterans. When he graduated, in two years, he was taken on the staff of First Denominational Church in Lakeport as a "minister of extension." In that rapidly expanding area in which the city was reaching out toward the campus of the small but growing Hynes Heights University, Farley, with the help of members released from the rolls of First Church, founded the Hynes Heights Denominational Church. After two years in a public-school building, the new congregation built its sanctuary with the help of a loan from the denomination. During what we remember as the pious ("Return to Religion") fifties the new congregation grew and flourished. Farley stayed with it for fifteen years and then, to the real distress of Hynes Heights, accepted the call of a small-town congregation about a hundred miles away, explaining that he coveted release from the pressures of suburban living in the booming sixties. He was a serious man, quietly eloquent and quite unlike the typical public relations–oriented "extension" pastor. He was greatly loved by the older members of Hynes Heights, and the church was glad to let its entire ministerial staff go each July, that the city-bound might once again enjoy the ministry of the Reverend Fred Farley. With his wife, who would spend the month shopping and attending concerts, Farley moved into the parsonage. He himself spent the month reading at the university library. Some parishioners did not let traveling many miles from vacation homes deter them from coming in for at least one Sunday in July to "hear Fred." When Willie Mae McNee died, there was no question of recalling any of the ministerial staff from some far corner of vacationland. Her friends among the elders rightly believed it to be eminently fitting that the Reverend Fred Farley should conduct the memorial service.

Mr. Farley was well aware of the melancholy events that had occurred the preceding late summer and early autumn. During his ministry in Hynes Heights he had often frequented the university library. Toward the end, he had been a part-time instructor in the small religious studies department. He knew Irene McFall and J. L. Brandywine, although they were not conspicuous by their presence in any church. Dan Sweeney was a Roman Catholic and relatively new in the community. Farley had never met him personally. But Ed Marsden was a member of the church, not as faithful in attendance as his wife, but neither was he merely a nominal member. He especially appreciated Fred Farley's thoughtful, studious, and rather quiet sermons, and was rather more faithful in church attendance during July (if he happened to be in the city) than at other times.

Farley was, of course, very angry about the treatment that Mrs. McNee had received in the last year of her life. His personal acquaintance with the late Tom McNee had been limited to social intercourse and philosophical disputation (what would now be called "rapping"). If he had lived in a village, Tom McNee would have been called the village atheist. Farley was not at all interested in whether or not there was any substance to the McFall blackmail charges. Whatever lay buried in the dim Scottish past of Thomas McNee did not justify the cruel attack on Willie Mae, a blackmail attack designed to drive her from the district and abandon her home. By this time there was no question of the University taking over the McNee residence in the near future. The blackmail had backfired. Irene McFall resigned all her positions on the boards and and committees of the University and moved away, nobody knew or cared where. So, with Brandy-wine's death, only Marsden was left of those who had become involved in the miserable plot. The president was quietly and somewhat pathetically slipping toward his retirement. Even before he stopped administrative breathing, the carrion hovered over the carcass, and the struggle for the succession began with whispers and knowing nods. The southward expansion of the University had been stopped in its tracks by the McNee house. By this time environmental concerns and a rising skepticism about education slowed all expansion programs to a twitching crawl. The plotters had indeed had their reward. Nevertheless, the Reverend Fred Farley believed it was necessary for him to set the whole wicked incident in the light of the Word of God.

He first thought to address the incident, which had become a *cause célèbre* in the community, at the funeral. After all, it was not an ordinary funeral with next-of-kin mourners. Both Dr. Marsden and Mr. Sweeney would likely be there, as well as other members of the academic community, many of whom had identified themselves with the expansion drive and had made little effort to conceal their annoyed amusement at Mrs. McNee's stubborn resistance. But he quickly decided against this. For at this service, the really important members of the congregation would be Mrs. McNee's fellow founding members of the congregation— senior citizens not far themselves from the place to which she had gone. So the service was short on sermon and eulogy, and long on scriptures and prayers of hope and comfort. It was a service that was much appreciated, not least by Dan Sweeney, who did not often stray from his own fold.

But Farley believed himself to be led to speak to the University-McNee conflict and confrontation on the Sunday following the funeral. He resisted this strong impulse for awhile, wondering whether it would not be, after all, flogging a dead horse. Mrs. McNee and Mr. Brandywine were dead, Dr. McFall was far from the scene, and there seemed to be little point in exacerbating the guilt feeling being endured by Dr. Marsden. He then remembered how late Elijah arrived in the vineyard of Naboth the Jezreelite and, in a kind of flash, the sermon title came to him: "Naboth's Vineyard is now Located in Hynes Heights." He did not seek sensationalism, but he did want the parish and the academic community to reflect on what had happened. He saw a "dynamic analogy" [1] between what had happened in Jezreel twenty-seven hundred years ago and what had just come to pass in Lakeport. His basic theological conviction was that the same Lord of history was present and active in both places, and that where he is present in judgment, he is also present in grace.

The preacher saw three possible approaches to the scripture and the theme. He could read the lesson and at sermon time speak to the contemporary situation, and let the people see the analogy. In a sense this was Jesus' method. The word "parable" comes from a verbal form meaning "to throw alongside of." Jesus did not answer the question "Who is my neighbor?" with an exposi-

135

tion of Deuteronomy or Leviticus. It the present case, the story was at hand and did not have to be invented and imagined.

The second method is to move from the contemporary scene back to the Bible—from now to then. The advantages of this method is that the interest of the hearers is immediately engaged and, if the material is skillfully presented and the transistion to antiquity and scripture imaginatively effected, this interest can be sustained. The sermon ends strongly with an inherent appeal to the authority of the Bible.

Farley often used both of these methods, but this time he chose not to do so. He was afraid that he was too emotionally engaged here to be sure that he would not exhaust himself in anger and denunciation before he ever got off the streets of Lakeport and into the vineyard of Naboth. So, for better or worse, he decided to start with I Kings 21 and move into Hynes Heights. He felt that the parallel was sufficiently close that his hearers would be aware of his purpose from the beginning, and there was little danger of losing them in a preliminary exegetical excursion.

During the week, Farley was greatly tempted to speculate on whether or not Dr. Marsden would be present and, if so, how this would influence his choice of words and tone of voice. He decided to ignore Marsden. There was no point in adding weight to his burden. Nor should the president be singled out for special censure in a society that had made a god of growth and development—a society whose golden calf was Education. Ed Marsden may have been Aaron, but the people had demanded the golden calf. He was but one idolater among the many.

Farley always planned his service carefully in connection with the sermon. Even a sermon addressed in prophetic judgment to an immediate situation is part of an act of worship—it is not a lecture or a political harangue. It is the Word of God uttered in its cultic setting. The prophet must not forget that he is also pastor, and functions as priest. In the summer season, the service at Hynes Heights was quite simple, shorn of choral theatrics and kindergarten capers.

ORDER OF WORSHIP

Opening Statement: Seek ye the Lord
          while he may be found,
       call ye upon him
          while he is near.
       Let the wicked forsake his
          way,
             and the unrighteous
             man his thoughts:
       and let him return unto the
          Lord,
             and he will have mercy
             upon him;

137

and to our God,
> for he will abundantly pardon.

[Isa. 55:6-7]

Prayer of Invocation:

Almighty God, unto whom all hearts are open, all desires known, and from whom no secrets are hid; Cleanse the thoughts of our hearts by the inspiration of thy Holy Spirit, that we may perfectly love thee, and worthily magnify thy holy Name; through Christ our Lord. *Amen.*

The Lord's Prayer.

Hymn of Praise:

The Lord is King! Lift up up your voice

Prayer of Confession:

People: Father, we have abused your world, and misused our abilities.

We have worshipped power and wealth, and have not sought your kingdom.

We have seen need in distant places, but have not responded here at home.

Even now, in your house,

our motives are mixed
and our wills are weak.
Lord, forgive us all our mis-
deeds; reshape our lives
from today; fulfill your plan
through us.

Leader: May God's love con-
quer us; may Christ's mercy
restore us; may the Spirit's
power fill us.

People: Amen.[2]

Statement of Assurance:

If we confess our sins, he
is faithful and just to forgive us our sins and to
cleanse us from all unrigh-
teousness.

Old Testament Lesson: I Kings 21:1-24.

Quartet: (a simple Psalm setting)
New Testament Lesson: Luke 10:25-37.

Prayers of Thanksgiving, Petition, and Interces-
sion.

Hymn: We have not known thee as we ought

Sermon: *"Naboth's Vineyard Is Now Located in
Hynes Heights"*

Offertory.

Hymn: Jesus shall reign where'er the sun

Benediction: The grace of our Lord
                            Jesus Christ, the love of God,
                            the fellowship of the Holy
                            Spirit, be with us all now
                            and evermore. *Amen.*

The parts of the service that occasioned Farley
some anxiety were the musical number and the
final hymn. He did not want the Old Testament
lesson to be followed with "In the Garden" type of
sentimental *Kitsch.* So he got in touch with the
guest musical director and tactfully arranged that
the quartet, which was on duty that summer Sunday, should offer a simple Psalm setting. It was not
entirely appropriate to the theme, but it was strong
and scriptural and not glaringly unfitting. For the
last hymn, he departed from the usual gospel invitation motif for the strong statement of the
coming victory of Christ expressed in Isaac
Watts' familiar words. The choice of the New
Testament passage seemed obvious to Farley. At
the heart of the Ahab-Naboth confrontation is the
question of the identity of my neighbor.

In his own parish, Farley generally followed
the themes of the Christian year. But he felt free
to depart and address himself to an urgent situation, as he was doing here in Hynes Heights. His
sermons became shorter as he grew older and

wiser. He realized that the modern congregation, which is also the television audience, is not used to long, lecture-like discussions. Twenty-five minutes had shrunk to somewhere between twelve and fifteen. He usually spoke without notes after careful preparation, but when liable to become involved in controversy, he was careful to read closely from a full manuscript. It was important to know exactly what he had said, not what he was remembered to have said. So we are fortunate to have the full text of this sermon.

Naboth's Vineyard Is Now Located in Hynes Heights

"There was none who sold himself to do what was evil in the sight of the Lord like Ahab, whom Jezebel his wife incited." We remember King Ahab in the light of this terrible judgment. We remember him as the adversary of the Lord's champion, the prophet Elijah. It is a dark memory. We think of him as a bad king, influenced by a wicked wife. This is not entirely fair to him and his record as the leader of Israel. In some ways he was a wise king. He recognized the threat of Damascus and its expansionary king Benhadad, and he successfully kept his little nation from invasion. He was aware of the far greater threat of Assyria, and was a leader in a coalition of small states which saved them from being smashed by this fierce aggressor. He realized the folly of continued border wars with the sister Hebrew state of Judah, and formed an alliance with her king Jehoshaphat. He continued his father's policy of fortifying the splendid and strategically functional capital city of Samaria. His father, Omri, had married him to the princess Jezebel of Tyre, and in this way an association was formed which, it was hoped, would open Israel up to the Mediterranean trade of the Phoenicians and ultimately the culture of the isles of Greece and Europe. It can be argued that Omri and his son Ahab conceived and executed wise, prudent, even imaginative policies, which saved their nation from internal disintegration and external threat, and enabled it to survive for a century more.

Ahab and his family, moreover, were far from pagan. His children, Ahaziah and Jehoram, were named in honor of the Lord God of Israel. His reluctance to seize the land of Naboth, his respect for the Lord's prophet, his remorse after Naboth's death, all showed that he was by no means totally alienated from the faith of his fathers and the Israelite way of life. The voice of conscience was not entirely stilled by the siren songs of ambition and progress which came to him through the voice of his queen.

Yet, in the balance of the history of the people of God, Ahab is weighed and found to be fatally lacking. His political wisdom and military courage did not outweigh his seduction by Jezebel into tolerance for the way of the world around him. His people had worshiped the stern desert God, the Lord of Israel, who was the giver of all good gifts—life, produce, progeny, prosperity, peace. He had delivered his people from slavery in Egypt long ago. He had led them across the desert and into the promised land, driving their enemies from before them. His covenant with them demanded of them, in exchange for his protection, an exclusive loyalty; for he said: "You shall have no other gods before me—I am a jealous God."

Now this was nonsense in the eyes of Jezebel and the culture which she represented. The religion of Canaan saw the divine power inherent in the world, in its biological vitality, its amazing beauty and variety. The king and the state are part of this divine order. Her religion was basically a process religion—confidence in, and identification with, the divine power inherent in nature and history. For a prince or a king, who stood somehow near the apex of all this, to be another servant of a jealous god, was absurd to her.

The other part of Israel's ancient covenant had to do with the community. "You shall love your neighbor as yourself." Not even the king could overrun the rights of a free Israelite citizen. One of the most important of these was the right of the citizen and his family to hold their own land in stewardship for the Lord, who is the ultimate

143

owner of all. The land is his. "The silver and the gold" are his "and the cattle upon a thousand hills." But Jezebel was part of the way of the world. Ahab's tragedy was that the temptation incarnate in her proved stronger than the voice that called from Sinai: "You shall love the Lord your God . . . and your neighbor as yourself." It is neither the first nor the last time that the call of the world has been more persuasive, its vision more alluring.

> . . . The world is ever near;
> I see the sights that dazzle,
> The tempting sounds I hear;
> My foes are ever near me,
> Around me and within . . .

Ahab's family had come from the town of Jezreel. After his father, Omri, had purchased the hill of Samaria, much time had to be spent building that capital. But Omri and his children maintained their family residence in the lovely town of Jezreel; there they lived when political and military affairs did not call them elsewhere. And it was in Jezreel that Jezebel and her royal, reigning son were to meet a bloody and vicious death in the coup that wiped out their dynasty. But all this is in the future. Ahab, at the height of his power, is enlarging and developing the royal properties in Jezreel. Right in the line of development is the vineyard of Naboth, an Israelite freeman. By the

144

law of Israel, there is nothing that even the king can do if Naboth refuses to trade or sell his property. The king—though sulking, sullen, and disappointed—does not see any alternative but to accept the verdict. But in the society from which Jezebel comes, such scruples do not stand in the way of the royal will. So in one cruel and lying stroke she brings about Naboth's judicial murder and leaves his land for the king to claim. She says, almost contemptuously, to her whining husband: "Go down and possess the vineyard of Naboth the Jezreelite, for he is no longer alive, he is dead."

Here in the suburb of Hynes Heights, in the city of Lakeport, Naboth's vineyard once again stood in the way of a royal development. For in our culture, Education is king, and we are all justly proud of our fine institution of higher learning. We would like to see the story of its development come to a fitting climax in an opening night in the splendid theater-auditorium that has been planned. Even those of us who live here no longer, look back with pride and happiness to the little college that served us and our children. We are indeed proud to have been associated with its growth in numbers, wealth, and reputation. We covet for it a still grander future. But the copybook which records the story of Hynes Heights University has been blotted red, not with the red ink of financial disaster, but with the red lifeblood

145

of Willie Mae McNee, whom we buried last Thursday. Mrs. McNee was not young. She might well have died last Monday in any case. But we could have let her die with dignity, in her own home, surrounded by the furnishings and trinkets of her past and the memories of her beloved husband. Jesus said to us: "The sabbath was made for man, not man for the sabbath." He also said, pointing to the holy temple: "Not one stone will stand upon another." The kingdom of God does not stand with the standing of any institution, any structure —however sacred. The reign of God is not in church or palace, but in the hearts of people. We can serve the cause of truth and beauty, and so serve God, by building fine institutions like Hynes Heights University. I would not put down the work of any, including Dr. McFall and the late Mr. Brandywine, who labored long and gave much to make it what it is today. But last autumn, Naboth, standing forlornly on his small plot of land and stubbornly on his God-given rights, lived again in Willie Mae McNee. Perhaps she seemed pathetic in the eyes of the world, but she stood bravely and stubbornly for her own right, defying that most sacred of our Great Society cows: Education. It is people like Naboth and Willie Mae that the kingdom of God is all about. Jesus spoke of "these little ones who believe in me" and described in rather extreme terms and not very nice language the fate of those who make them

146

stumble. They would be lucky, he said, if all that happened to them is that they are thrown into the sea with a millstone around their necks.

The prophet Elijah sets foot on Naboth's vineyard too late to be of any help. The dire deed is done. All he can do now is announce the Word of the Lord. Ahab and Jezebel will die violent deaths and be denied honorable and seemly burials. The dogs will lick their blood. In the case of Ahab, he felt remorse and was granted an honorable death in battle, although he was not buried until the dogs licked the blood that dropped from his chariot in Samaria, and the harlots washed themselves in it. And not long thereafter his queen and his two sons—the whole promising dynasty—came to an inglorious end, not far from where Naboth's vineyard stood.

It is indeed a word of judgment. Such a word the prophets bring. In this service today our last words will be about grace and love and fellowship —but even in that context we cannot forbear to speak the word of judgment. For there can be no grace and love and fellowship without judgment. If the cruelties perpetrated on the Naboths and Willie Maes go unnoticed in an uncaring universe, there can be no victory of truth and goodness and there is no God whose grace a thinking person would covet. But Jezreel, and Auschwitz, and 2001 University Lane are not the last word. The scene in Jezreel was a cruel scene. There was no token of grace apparent there. In the Christian concern of Mr. Dan Sweeney, we did have a token of grace here. And in the continued presence, a rather absurd presence, of the little house at 2001 University Lane, we may for a long time yet have a symbol that speaks of the emptiness of human plans, however grand, which set aside the inalienable rights of the least of these little ones who believe in the Lord in whose name we are gathered. Amen.

7 CAN The MODERN ChRISTIAN PREACHER SPEAK ThROUGH The ANCIENT hEBREW PROPHETS?

The creative period of Hebrew prophecy oc-curred between the career of Elijah and the end of the ministry of Jeremiah (about 860–580 B.C.).[1] There were many prophets during this time, and they spoke differing words in varied tones, ac-cording to their own personalities and the situa-tions that they addressed. Yet three general state-ments can be made about their words to Israel.

1. Each prophet spoke the Word of the Lord directly to the situation in which he found him-

self. His voice found utterance in a moment of crisis in the life of Israel. The prophetic word is a word to a place, a people, and a season. As Gerhard von Rad put it, in what is probably the most enlightening study we have of Old Testament prophecy:

> The word that came on each occasion is not to be set alongside the rest of the words of Jahweh, so that it is only in the synthesis that it yields something like the message the prophet has to announce; on the contrary, for the person concerned it is the complete word of God, and has no need of tacit supplementation by other words which the prophet had already spoken on other occasions.[2]

Great violence is therefore done to the very genius of Hebrew prophecy if we seek to systematize it into a "doctrine of the prophets," then take this abstracted doctrine as generalized theological and moral instruction applicable to quite different life situations. We must not infer from Jeremiah that a besieged nation ought never to resist an aggressor (Jer. 34:1, 2), or from Isaiah that a small nation should never ally itself with a great power (Isa. 30:1-22). Each of these words is a Word of God appropriate to a given situation, and not automatically transferable to other situations.

2. The ancient Hebrew prophets were not individualistic. They did not seek person-by-person

conversion and reformation in the hope that the whole society would be delivered by the wholeness of each person in it, if that could be achieved. When they addressed individuals it was an address to representative persons, usually kings and commanders, whose deeds and destiny incorporated the deeds and destiny of all Israel. The prophets were not evangelists in the modern sense, preaching for "decisions" by persons.

3. The great preexilic prophets were prophets of doom.[3] An editor of the Elijah stories predicted the end of Ahab and the Omride dynasty (I Kings 21:22). Hosea saw no improvement in the junta whose coup destroyed the Omrides and thus fulfilled the word of Elijah (Hosea 1:4-5). Micah and Jeremiah, without equivocation, proclaimed the very end of the elect nation itself (Mic. 3:12; Jer. 7:15, 32-33). This vision of the nation's end as a historical community mushroomed like an atomic cloud into a proclamation of cosmic, cataclysmic doom.

> I looked on the earth, and lo, it was waste and void;
> and to the heavens, and they had no light.
> I looked on the mountains, and lo, they were quaking,
> and all the hills moved to and fro.
> I looked, and lo, there was no man,
> and all the birds of the air had fled.
> I looked, and lo, the fruitful land was a desert,
> and all its cities were laid in ruins
> before the Lord, before his fierce anger. . . .

> For this the earth shall mourn,
>   and the heavens above be black;
> for I have spoken, I have purposed;
>   I have not relented nor will I turn back.
>   [Jer. 4: 23-26, 28 RSV]

The idea of a surviving remnant, first revealed to Elijah (I Kings 19:18), and later dramatized by Isaiah in the naming of one of his sons (Isa. 7:3, then developed in 6:13 and 10:20-23), is not really a prophecy of hope. The remnant is that pathetic, miserable, and insignificant part of a nation that survives a terrible invasion—what is left in the scorched-earth destruction of a community, its population, and its means of existence.[4]

These three features of the prophetic message— and I must emphasize that they are of the very essence of the form—make use of the prophetic oracles in modern preaching a hazardous business. That our situation is vastly different in the global village of the late twentieth century, in the wake of geometrically accelerated technological and communications revolutions, is the most obvious of truisms. Moreover, human nature and the human situation are perceived in a very different manner. For we are the heirs of the Enlightenment—of the Romantic movement in art and aesthetics, and liberalism in politics—and thus we are accustomed to an emphasis on the individual in all things, including, of course, religion. It would have been impossible for an ancient Is-

152

raelite to envisage a religious community, a "church," made up of individuals who are voluntarily associated, and that church separate from the nation. Nor do those two crucial facets of modern liberalism—the concept that the essence of man is his freedom, and the idea of progress —have any place whatever in Old Testament thought.

This is not to say that the covenant teachers of ancient Israel forgot or despised the individual person. The story of Naboth itself stands as witness to their concern for "one of the least of these little ones" who belong to the community. But the idea of the individual person being "saved" out of a lost community, or of the salvation of the community being dependent upon the totality of right "decisions" by separate persons, is one that was only occasionally entertained at the periphery of Old Testament teaching (e.g., Ezek. 18:1-32).

To say that the preexilic Old Testament prophets were, by and large, prophets of doom is not to liken them to the modern preacher who exhorts his congregation and his society to reform in morals and religion lest our civilization follow in the wake of its departed predecessors. A familiar homiletical example or type is the Roman empire, which is alleged to have fallen because of internal moral disintegration. One wonders whether the human lot would be better today had the Romans so believed and behaved that their splendid tyranny would have survived the centuries! Why is it a bad thing that Rome fell? No; such moralizing was not the burden of the prophetic judgment. For the prophet proclaimed the full end of Israel as a palpable historical community:

I have forsaken my house,
  I have abandoned my heritage;
I have given the beloved of my soul
  into the hands of her enemies.
                    [Jer. 12:7 RSV]

Zion shall be plowed as a field;
Jerusalem shall become a heap of
    ruins,
  and the mountain of the house a
  wooded height.
                    [Mic. 3:12 RSV]

The God of Israel is free, even of Israel! He is not bound by any people or institution, however venerable and sacred. To comprehend this about the prophetic message does not necessarily entitle us to proclaim the end of Christendom. But it does save us from using the prophetic judgments as a basis for scolding our people into what we believe to be better faith and doctrine.

There are, then, profound discontinuities between the vision of human nature and destiny that informs the prophetic world of Israel, and the vision that informs us in modern Christian civilization. We must be aware of these discontinuities;

154

they must force us to ask two questions before using the prophetic oracles as the basis of our proclamation and paraenesis. The first question is: Is the modern appreciation of human nature and the human situation necessarily correct? Or, to put the same thing the other way: must we assume that the biblical comprehension has been superseded? If we do not answer this question, whichever way it is put, in the negative, then surely we have forfeited the right to claim that the Bible is the source of authority for faith and life. So if we stand in the tradition of biblical authority, we are still saying, with the teachers of Israel, that God addresses us in our specific situation; he commands us where we are, not with general advice, but with concrete commandments. We must affirm that we are bound up together in the bundle of life, death, and eternity, and so all distinctions between "individual salvation" and "social gospel" arise from a modernism that is alien to the Bible. And, finally, the God whom we serve and before whom we stand as prophets, is truly free—he is free of us! The issue of his coming victory in the universe is not conditioned by the perpetuation of our churches, our nation, our economic system, our families, our forms of worship, our existence in time!

The second question is: In admitting the profound discontinuity between the "strange" world of the Bible and the world of modern megalopolis, are we saying that there are no abiding or recurring elements in the human situation and the divine-human encounter? Is there no analogy to be perceived in what happened twenty-eight centuries ago in Jezreel, and what happens in the high-rise offices and dwellings of the Great Society, along its throughways and in its factories, its churches, its hospitals, schools, and universities? To find the analogy, without ignoring the discontinuities, is the hermeneutical task that must be undertaken by whoever it is that seeks to speak to our time in the name and the spirit of the prophets of Israel.

It could be argued that the universal adult franchise has made the prophetic word and style superfluous in the modern democratic state. Perhaps the prolix literary prophesying and consequent exile of a Solzhenitsyn is necessary in the Soviet Union, even as the word, deed, and death of a Bonhoeffer were required in Nazi Germany. If citizens of the democracies are concerned with justice and mercy in public affairs, they can and should get involved in the political process. After all, we choose our Ahabs. The events of August, 1974, in the United States showed that the power of the grandest of them all can be brought to an end. For power resides in the people who give it and can take it away.

This argument becomes less persuasive as the social order with its supporting technology becomes more complicated and the infrastructures of its power more pervasive, even as they become more and more invisible. Does the termination of the incumbency of a president or a prime minister, the electoral overthrow of a given parliament or congress, make a significant change in the real world of power? Is the power of an international consortium of oil companies and sheikdoms to determine whether the poor of the nations shall be cold or warm in wintertime any different under a Ford than it was under a Nixon? Would there be any real difference under a Jackson or a Mondale? Will the result of an election determine the quality of shelter and the amount of food that the poor receive? What hope does the electoral victory of any party hold for the people of the Belfast slums or the embattled ghettos of Londonderry?

Three-digit inflation was probably the chief reason for the overthrow of the legitimate Marxist government of Chile. Three-digit inflation continues under the totalitarian junta which replaced it. It would seem that often even a 180-degree turn in the political helm makes no difference, at least in the short term.

But it would be unnecessarily cynical to deny that the integrity of the persons who govern, and the public philosophy which motivates them, make no difference in the long run. The political burden of the Christian citizen is surely to work for the election of persons of good will who promote a

157

public philosophy consonant with love of God and love of neighbor.

But the prophetic word, deed, and style confront the ruler and the ruling class that is in power now, when issues of justice and mercy are immediately at stake, when injustice and cruelty are being done or are about to be done. The Supreme Court can order that the racial integration of schools proceed with "all deliberate speed," and legislatures can pass laws to implement such a *torah* (direction). If existing legislatures refuse to do this, new legislators must be elected. In the meantime, blood is shed and bones are broken on the streets of south Boston. That such is happening while these words are being written, and will perhaps be forgotten when they are read, only indicates how immediate, how *ad hoc* is the very genius of prophecy, which never deals in abstractions and doctrines.

The prophetic event (incorporating word, deed, and style in this expression) is a happening which confronts existing principalities and powers with the demand for justice and mercy now, or pronounces judgment when injustice or cruelty has irrevocably occurred. It is Meredith on the steps of "Ole Miss"; it is Martin Luther King dead on a Memphis balcony; it is minister, nun, and social worker marching together on the road to Montgomery. Among Old Testament scholars there is academic controversy as to whether the prophets

158

were cultic or secular, priestly or lay. It is very likely that then, as now, they are "both-and," not "either-or"! The prophetic event, now as in Old Testament times, is an immediate address to a public issue demanding justice and mercy, or it is a word of judgment on a deed done. It is a "prophecy of doom" in that the continuity of existing institutions, however sacred, is never the ultimate concern of the prophet. Church and nation exist to serve man and God. The prophetic witness can thus be described as "irresponsible" and "irrelevant" if responsibility and relevance mean serving man through preserving his institutional ecology. The burning body of Jan Palach on the streets of Prague, kept quiet by the presence of the tanks and guns of the Soviet Union, was a supremely irrelevant, and perhaps irresponsible, event. It was nonetheless a word and deed of prophetic power.

A Gulf of Tonkin congressional resolution may seek to legitimize the continued prosecution of an illegal war. The citizen who accepts the implication of this statement must make it his political duty to elect (or become) a legislator who will annul the resolution and seek to make the passage of another like it impossible. In the meantime myriads on both sides, and on neither, will die in a war-torn land. The prophet then does not wait for a new legislature. The only response he can make is the prophetic word and deed: blood poured on the draft card, self-inflicted exile on alien soil, the honored name now a number on a prison shirt, the sound of marching feet on moratorium day, the voice of Senator McCarthy in the New Hampshire hills, the lonely ordeal of the pastor whose conviction means that the son of his own elder has died in vain. The prophetic burden is never a picnic hamper:

> For whenever I speak, I cry out,
>   I shout, "Violence and destruction!"
> For the word of the Lord has become for me
>   a reproach and a derision all day long.
> [Jer. 20:8 RSV]

When Elijah set foot in Naboth's vineyard, the terrible wrong done could not be set right—Naboth was dead and his land expropriated. The prophetic word of God is not silenced because the deed is irrevocably done and cannot be undone; the prophetic word becomes a word of judgment —and only a word of judgment.

On Sunday, September 8, 1974, President Gerald R. Ford, invoking his constitutional power to pardon and "acting as a humble servant of God" granted a "full, free and absolute pardon" to his predecessor "for all offenses against the United States which he, Richard Nixon, has committed, or may have committed or taken part in" during the period of his incumbency. No one disputes the president's power to pardon. It was a deed of obvious constitutional propriety and, in a very real way, was prophetic in its efficacy, for it is a word that, once spoken, accomplishes its purpose (Isa. 55:11). The source of the authority, however, is not the word of God, but the constitution of the United States of America which, however venerable and normally binding, is a word of men. Thus the act, which cannot be withdrawn or modified, is a fit subject for the prophetic judgment. Did the president "do justly and love mercy and walk humbly with his God" or did he, in showing mercy to one man and his family, fail to uphold his own oath to execute the law without partiality?

The Reverend Doctor Duncan Littlefair, of Grand Rapids, Michigan, a man who does not normally find his distinguished neighbor's political views congenial, saw in the pardon a token of grace, and was quick to bless the deed: "There was nothing dark or dishonorable about Ford's motives in pardoning Richard Nixon. . . . 'Forgive when you can. Mercy and forgiveness cannot be weighed, measured and balanced and counted—they must always be free, unearned and undeserved." [5]

Neither the general public (if the polls are to be believed) nor some prominent spokesmen of the church would support Dr. Littlefair in his word of blessing. The *Christian Century* was especially stern in its reaction to the pardon:

161

President Ford has made a decision that damages our judicial process, gives preferential treatment to one man over thousands, and further taints the office he holds with the suspicion that his action stemmed from some ulterior motive which may now be forever buried by the single stroke of that pardoning pen. Either we have a President who makes unwise political decisions when he is reached at a sensitive point, or we have a President who continues the Watergate cover-up.[6]

Which is the true prophetic word here—the blessing or the cursing? Who can tell "at this point in time"! We do indeed have a God who "delighteth in mercy," but is pardon receivable unless fault be acknowledged? What about pardon for Watergate conspirators already indicted, convicted and, in some cases, under detention? Is it irrelevant to ask why persons who appealed to the (for them) higher law of conscience in flouting the law of the land should be forever exiles unless they acknowledge guilt and earn their homecoming? Why should pardon be granted to the chief magistrate, sworn to uphold the law, and amnesty be denied them? The sentence against Ahab was mitigated and mercy shown when he "humbled himself" before God and acknowledged the validity of the prophetic sentence against him (I Kings 21:29).

Examples of public situations which call for the prophetic judgment can be multiplied forever,

162

down the centuries and around the world. What is the prophetic word for Canadians, whose native people, protesting against historic injustice, disturbed the opening of Parliament with a demonstration that generated some mild violence in the fall of 1974? What is the prophetic word for South Africa and Rhodesia, and, across the color and culture line, for Zambia and Uganda? What word is addressed to the interconfessional fratricide of Ulster; what deed can mirror the horror of Christians at war one with another? The very genius of the prophetic word, deed, and style is that it is unique in the situation in which it is uttered. No one from afar in space and time can put God's word in the mouth of the prophet. But that word is always recognized for its immediacy, its public nature, and its independence from making the perpetuation of any ecclesiastical or political institution a matter of ultimate concern.

The God of Israel, who moves in the events of human history, has left his footprints particularly plain in the deeds and words of his servants the prophets. It is the conviction of Christian faith that to follow the path of those footprints will bring us to the place where we come into his very presence in the person of Jesus Christ. In his life, death, and living again, and in his word, the prophetic words of judgment and grace, promise and fulfillment, chastisement and healing, death and resurrection are spoken clearly for those who

163

have ears to hear. "In many and various ways, God spoke of old to our fathers by the prophets; but in these last days he has spoken to us by a Son . . ." (Heb. 1:1-2 RSV). Yet in the last word of the last days the earlier words are neither obscured nor nullified, nor even rendered preliminary and partial. They are rather guaranteed and illuminated by the one who came not to destroy, but to fulfill, the law and the prophets.

NOTES

1. The Development of the Elijah Saga Cycle

1. By classical prophets is meant those who gave their names to books of the Bible: Isaiah, Jeremiah, Ezekiel and the twelve minor prophets. Sometimes these are miscalled writing prophets. It is very likely that Amos, for instance, was illiterate.

2. Even this note at I Kings 17:1 is obscure. The Hebrew text reads: "Now Elijah the Tishbite, from the settlers of Gilead . . ." The Greek translation reads: "Now Elijah the prophet the Tishbite, from Tishbe of Gilead . . ." No doubt Elijah came from Gilead, across the Jordan from Samaria.

3. My dates follow those adopted in J. Bright, *A History of Israel* (Philadelphia: Westminster Press, 1959), pp. 461 ff. Unless otherwise specified the dates are all B.C.

4. *Yahweh* is the usual spelling adopted for the covenant name of the God of Israel. In the Hebrew Bible his name was spelled YHWH. Because, for reasons of reverence, the name was not pronounced, the vocalization has to be conjectured Much ink has been spilled in the discussion of what this name originally meant. We have no way of knowing.

5. In the recitation accompanying the gift of the first-fruits, Deut. 26:4-11, this "salvation history" is recited by the Israelite worshiper.

6. In the holy war, neither prisoners nor booty are to be taken. All is to be devoted to destruction, a burnt offering to Yahweh: Josh. 6:17, 18, etc.

7. John Gray, *I & II Kings* (London: SCM Press, 1964), pp. 379-80, thinks the word translated "ravens" should be "Arabs." In the Hebrew language only consonants are used in writing. The same consonants with differing vowel points will yield "ravens" and "Arabs." The early Greek translation, following a Hebrew text without vowels, however, understood the Hebrew word in question to be "ravens."

8. This story is retold, with greater detail and sense of the marvelous, about Elijah's successor Elisha, in II Kings 4:18-37.

9. This distinction between historically significant stories of the prophets and pious legends is made in Georg Fohrer's study of the prophet, *Elia* (Zurich: Zwingi Verlag, 2nd ed., 1968).

10. Often, as in Whittier's famous hymn, the "still small voice" represents a serene, mystical experience of God and peace. But here the voice of God commands the prophet to instigate a brutal blood purge.

11. In the Greek translation, the story of Naboth is chap. 20, and thus it is placed with the rest of the prophetic stories of Elijah; and the two battle accounts, chaps. 20 and 22 in the Hebrew Bible, are gathered together at the end of the book. The editor of I Kings in the Hebrew Bible had, however, separated the Naboth story from the others to connect the prediction of Elijah directly with the last

battle of Arab in chap. 22. Editorial arrangements in the Bible serve, often, a didactic or theological purpose.

2. The Search for the Historical Elijah

1. Martin Noth, *The History of Israel,* rev. trans. (New York: Harper, 1960), p. 42.

2. H. G. May and B. M. Metzger, eds., *The Oxford Annotated Bible* (New York: Oxford University Press, 1962), n. on p. 447.

3. The "judges" who, despite their title, were military deliverers rather than judicial figures, were raised up in moments of crisis to lead the Israelite tribes in the days between the settlement in Canaan and the establishment of the monarchy. They were charismatic figures, raised up for the crisis. They could not pass on their authority to sons or appointed successors.

4. The "foreign policy" of Judah's greatest prophet in the Assyrian period was essentially isolationist. Isaiah advised Judah's kings to keep her from external entanglements (*e.g.,* Isa. 7:10 ff. and 30:1-5) and seek deliverance in quiet confidence in Yahweh's protection (Isa. 30:15).

5. I Kings 15:26, 34, etc. The deuteronomic historian makes this comment on all of Israel's unfortunate kings.

6. Bright, *A History of Israel,* p. 219.

7. Athaliah, if she was Ahab's daughter, must have been his daughter by a marriage previous to his marriage with Jezebel. Possibly she was a younger sister.

8. J. B. Pritchard, ed., *The Ancient Near East, an Anthology of Texts and Pictures* (Princeton: Princeton University Press, 1958), p. 190.

9. J. A. Montgomery and H. S. Gehman, *A Critical and*

167

Exegetical Commentary on the Books of Kings (New York: Scribner's, 1951), pp. 284, 285. This great commentary was the last major work of Dr. Montgomery. After his death Dr. Gehman finished and edited the work. It is the last volume of the International Critical Commentary series.

10. W. F. Albright, *From the Stone Age to Christianity,* 2nd ed. (New York: Anchor Books; Doubleday, 1957), p. 307.

11. Gray, *I & II Kings,* p. 368.

12. Albright, *From The Stone Age to Christianity,* p. 307.

13. Pritchard, *The Ancient Near East,* pp. 209, 210.

14. Bright, *A History Of Israel,* p. 232.

15. The term Fertile Crescent describes the arc of land whose southern terminus is the Nile Valley; it goes north along the Mediterranean east coast, turns east, and descends to the gulf of Araq through the Tigris-Euphrates valley. At its southwestern end is Egypt, and at its eastern end is the site of the great Mesopotamian empires. Along its course were settlement, trade, and military routes. Small states like Judah and Israel were caught like nuts in a cracker between the great powers.

3. In the Vineyard of Naboth the Jezreelite

1. See discussion of I Kings 21:27-29 on p. 57.

2. Gray, *I & II Kings,* p. 45. See also J. D. Shenkel, *Chronology and Recensional Development in the Greek Text of Kings* (Cambridge: Harvard University Press, 1968), p. 88: "The story of Naboth's vineyard is completely devoid of chronological interest. This undoubtedly explains why the Hebrew text placed this story after the narrative of the anonymous prophet, reversing the order of the Greek text. The Greek arrangement is superior,

however, because it keeps all the stories about Elijah and Ahab together."

3. The problem of the locale of Naboth's vineyard and the events of chap. 21 is fully explored in B. D. Napier, "The Omrides of Jezreel," *Vetus Testamentum,* IX (1959), 366-78. Napier concludes, after much discussion, that the Omride home was Jezreel even after Samaria had been bought and its fortifications begun. He concluded that the events in chap. 21, as well as the story of the Jehu *coup d'état* in II Kings 9 and 10, all occurred in Jezreel.

4. Gray, *I & II Kings,* p. 438.

5. The year of jubilee occurs every half-century—after seven sabbaths of years.

6. Montgomery and Gehman, *A Critical and Exegetical Commentary,* p. 332.

7. Napier, "The Omrides of Jezreel," p. 368.

8. Montgomery and Gehman, *A Critical and Exegetical Commentary,* p. 332.

9. Gray, *I & II Kings,* pp. 442, 443. The theory here is that the Elijah and Elisha cycles were combined and included in a longer document, which may be styled "stories of the prophets"—which included accounts of many of the preclassical prophets.

10. Perhaps the definitive modern study of Elijah is Georg Fohrer's *Elia.* Fohrer finds four additions to the Naboth narrative in chap. 21 (pp. 28 and 29). He includes the judgment on Jezebel as an after-the-event prophecy, added to the Elijah narrative after the Jehu purge. Vss. 27-29 is also an after-the-event prophecy—the event being the death of Ahab in battle. Verses 21:20b-22, 24 comes from the redactor of the books of Kings who sees in Ahab's person the incarnation of the fate of the whole dynasty and uses expressions already employed in 14:10-11, and 16:3. In vss. 25 and 26 another commentator sees in Ahab's person and deeds a symptom of the growing apostasy of Israel. Fohrer sees two hands in these verses and says the Hebrew word used here for idols *(gillūlîm)* and the expression "to do abominably" *(tā'abh)* in Hifil) are characteristic of late postexilic times.

Fohrer concludes his study of chap. 21 with these words:

"All these additions show what an impression the narrative made on later generations and how deeply the person of Elijah had impressed itself on the mind [of the people]. Indeed it had a great deal to do with the sudden downfall of the reigning dynasty of Omri by the hand of Jehu."

4. How to Get Lost in Naboth's Vineyard

1. Ronald Knox, *A Spiritual Aeneid* (London: Burns Oates, new. ed., 1950), pp. 125 ff.

2. John Gray, *I and II Kings: A Commentary,* 2nd ed. (London: SCM Press, 1970).

3. John Bright, *The Authority of the Old Testament* (Nashville: Abingdon Press, 1967), pp. 131 ff.

4. *Ibid.,* pp. 58 ff.

5. *J. B.—a Play in Verse* (Boston: Houghton Mifflin, 1961).

6. Naboth's Vineyard Is Now Located in Hynes Heights

1. J. A. Sanders, *Torah and Canon* (Philadelphia: Fortress Press, 1972), p. xvi: "The believing community, whether synagogue or church, can find out what it is and what it ought to be by employing valid hermeneutic rules when reading the Bible. The believing community abuses the Bible whenever it seeks in it models for its morality, but

reads it with validity when it finds in the Bible mirrors for its identity. By dynamic analogy the community sees its current tensions, between what it is and what it ought to be, in the tensions which Israel and the early church also experienced."

2. This prayer of confession is taken from *The Hymnal* (Baptist Federation of Canada, 1973), where it is numbered #632. The prayer was written for *The Hymnal* by Dr. J. R. C. Perkin.

7. Can the Modern Christian Preacher Speak Through the Ancient Hebrew Prophets?

1. It can be argued, of course, that the creative period would go down to the time of the two prophets of exile and reconstruction—Ezekiel and II Isaiah.

2. *Old Testament Theology,* Vol. II: *The Theology of Israel's Prophetic Traditions,* trans, D. M. G. Stalker (Edinburgh and London: Oliver and Boyd, 1965), p. 88.

3. Among their words there are also oracles of hope (*e.g.,* Isa. 2:1-5; 11:1-9; Amos 9:8b-15, etc.) The position is here assumed that these oracles are generally later than the prophet whose name they bear. In any case the hope is not a historical hope for the future but is a promise of salvation beyond apocalyptic destruction.

4. von Rad, *Old Testament Theology,* II, 20, 21.

5. Quoted in Hugh Sidey, "The Presidency," *Time,* Oct. 7, 1974.

6. Editorial entitled "Another White House Either/or Dilemma," *The Christian Century,* Sept. 25, 1974, p. 867.

INDEX

173